Redefine Your Success in Sports, Business and Life Through Mindfulness

Mike Lee

THRIVE3
5510 West Bluemound Road
Milwaukee, WI
53208

MILWAUKEE | LOS ANGELES

J.P.

I hope the stories and
principles in this book
encourage and inspire you
to keep dreaming and
never settle. I'm grateful
for our friendship!

M2

Contents

BOOK III: Bring YOU to Life

Acknowledgments

One thing I've learned is that you have to have faith that on the other side of pain is greatness. And, many times we are so stuck in our heads that we need other people to mirror back to us the greatness that is within side all of us. Hidden under all the self-doubt, insecurities and sadness is a gift. You. Your truest most authentic self.

I'm not there yet, but through writing this book I've discovered a lot. It's the book I needed to read 15 years ago. And, it wouldn't have been possible without the love and support of so many people who gave their hearts, sweat and believed in me for the past 33 years. The authors that inspired me, my coaches, family, friends, yoga instructors, and meditation teachers.

First of all, my parents, Cindy and Ed Lee — Thank you for your unconditional love, teaching me to work and to have patience.

Luke Meier — thank you for all your support and belief in what we do. I am so lucky to have you and your understanding, beautiful wife who supports us as well. Your faith definitely gets me through some days. Brian Gryszkiewicz and Drew Windler for believing in this book and giving me the support to write it. Kyle Keranen and Ben Fischer for teaching our philosophy through the game.

Khadija McMahon — for challenging me, inspiring me and being my rock in times of both personal and professional struggles. You are an amazing human being.

Joshua Medcalf — for encouraging me to write this book, share my story and making me believe that it will impact thousands of people.

To all the parents who allowed me to coach your kids and be

a positive influence in their life.

Thank you to the following for inviting me to speak at your clinics, workout your players, or shining your light on me and empowering me to shine mine.

Brian Brinkerhoff (Full Court Basketball/Level X Hoops), Stephen Curry, Buzz Williams (Virginia Tech), Tommy Hulihan, Terry Fischer, Brian Vande Lune (Standfirm Baskebtall Academy), Joe Koeniczny (Columbus Catholic High School), Forrest Larson (Take it to the Rim), Eddie Andrist (University of Wisconsin-Stout), Kenny Atkinson (Atlanta Hawks), Bill Peterson (Erie Bayhawks), Dale Layer, Ike Wilson (Nike Playground Elite), Justin Litscher (Wisconsin Swing), Jason Jesperson (Wisconsin Playmakers), Joe Russom (Fox Valley Hustle), Jerry Petitgoue (WBCA/Cuba City High School), Steve Becker and Spencer Schulz (Athlete Peformance), Dave MacArthur (Colby High School, 1970-2006) Ganon Baker, Alan Stein (Stronger Team/DeMatha), Kevin Orr (Rice Lake High School), Andy Banasik (Prairie du Chien) Eric Oleszak, Brett Hirsch, and Tyler Schulz (Wisconsin Shooters), Kyle Manary (Nike Basketball), Drew Hanlen (Pure Sweat Basketball), Brian James (Northwestern University) Dee Brown (Sacramento Kings), Oties Epps (Evansville University), John Paul Crimi, Shayna Hiller.

THE DREAMERS

This book is for the dreamers. For those looking to discover the tools and mindset to uncover, unlock, and unleash their inner greatness.

The coach, athlete, and parent looking for a new way — a new way of happiness, inner peace and calm in this world of money, winning, and scholarships. For those looking to redefine success, on their terms, and create new meaning for their life and the people they lead and love.

Because when you really dig deep, you don't want success. You want the feeling that you THINK success is going to give you. Which, you'll learn, you can actually tap into right now. By falling in love with process — and ultimately, finding inner peace knowing that you did the best you could with what you had, to the best of your ability — you'll discover success.

It's for the coach who doesn't want to settle for back-to-back championships or the coach looking to win his first one. And, why transforming your players' minds and hearts is the way to get there.

The parent who truly wants the best for their kids and doesn't want to let society define what success means for them. For the parent who sees his child love something, but not knowing when to let go and let them explore the journey on their own.

The athlete who works harder, watches more film and spends

more time in the weight room than anyone else. But, is still looking for an edge.

The entrepreneur, executive, or leader who wants to take their organization to the next level. By taking the success principles — persistence, vision, and communication — and amplifying them through a higher level of awareness.

By reading this book, and putting the principles into action, you'll begin to tap into the power that already exists within you. A power that people like Kobe Bryant, Oprah Winfrey and Steve jobs used to elevate their craft to elite levels.

So...

Do you want to get to the next level, but find inner peace along the way?

Are you ready to UnTrain?

Let's begin.

BOOK I
MY JOURNEY

Chapter 1
THE DIAGNOSIS

"Based on the results of this survey, you are clinically depressed. Seek professional psychiatric care as soon as possible."

What? You have got to be kidding me. I wasn't depressed I told myself. Depressed was the goth kids wearing all black clothes, makeup and listening to Marilyn Manson and System of a Down. I sat there in my college dorm room, the fall of my freshman year at University of Wisconsin-Stout, in disbelief, yet with some sort of sense of relief.

My mind started to think back on all the times growing up, as early as 3rd or 4th grade, with my mom asking me:

"Michael, are you doing okay today?"

"I'm really worried about you, do you want to go talk to someone?"

"You look sad"

Back then, externally, everything seemed fine. I had loving parents, was attending a good school, and playing basketball. On the outside everything was great. But that was the challenge. I was so young I didn't know how to look inward.

My answer every single time was the same, "I'm fine."

Feelings
Inside
Not
Expressed

F.I.N.E. is damn right. I wasn't fine, I felt awful. I didn't want to play basketball, socialize, or do anything active. There were so many days when all I wanted to do was sleep. I always played it off as if my body was just too tired from all the work I put into basketball and I just needed rest. But in reality it was the depression that caused me to be so fatigued. In high school and college my friends would laugh when they'd come over at 12 or 1 p.m. on Saturdays and see me still sleeping.

"What is wrong with you? Get up! It's already past lunch!"

Finally, I at least knew what was going on and why I didn't want to go to basketball practice. I fell in love with the game in 3rd grade watching Jordan and the Bulls play against the Lakers, and now finally was at the point where I was at the point where I could experience and fulfill my dream.

To play college basketball.

No, it wasn't at Michigan, where I'd hoped to be after falling in love with Jalen Rose and the Fab Five — I even wore my dad's black dress socks before anyone else remotely close to us (in small-town central Wisconsin) started carrying the NIKE ones Jalen wore.

I'd have to beg my parents to rush home from church on Sundays to get catch the Fab Five with the games starting at 11 a.m. in Ann Arbor.

But, I was finally in college and able to compete in practice everyday against guys who were just as good or better than me. I stepped on the floor and learned something new almost every single day. It was a dream. Learning how to improve at something you love on a daily basis? It doesn't get a lot better than that. But, what I didn't know then, is that it's not about being the best.

It's about being YOUR best, while pursuing your potential doing something you love.

I didn't understand that it's not about perfection — it's about getting a little better everyday and falling in love with the process. But, my pursuit of perfection and success got the best of me when I got to college. Combine that with depression, defining yourself by what you do — not who you are — and I was on the road to nowhere fast.

Chapter 2

DROPPING OUT OF LOVE

I grew up in Marshfield, a small community in central Wisconsin, 3.5 hours away from both Minneapolis and Milwaukee. My first love was baseball, hitting balls from my dad and playing catch with my grandfather. Until the Bulls played the Lakers in the '91 finals, that's what I did. Soon, it changed.

My younger brother Shawn picked up the first issue ever of SLAM Magazine with Shawn Kemp on the cover, we fell in love with the Bulls, Michael Jordan, the Fab Five, and everything basketball. Street culture, sneakers, clothes, and of course, West Coast Gangsta Rap. I finally now know why my mom took away all my Snoop, Dre and Warren G Tapes that I got from my friend's older sister. With no Internet, cable TV and being 3.5 hours from any major city, it was a passion hard to fulfill. And, at times, I definitely got bored of it. Maybe I didn't love it as much as I say I did, and I'm not making excuses, but it's definitely tough to stay motivated when you think you're the best player in your area (even though I probably wasn't).

A note to coaches and parents: you can tell your players and kids all you want that they need to work harder and be better — but experience is king. Sometimes, you need to get your ass kicked.

I attended high school at Marshfield Columbus, a small

Catholic school with an enrollment of about 150 kids. Yep. That was my entire school, not my class. I played JV as a freshman and varsity from there out, winning back-to-back WISAA State and Conference Championships as a sophomore and junior.

Out of high school I was recruited by a couple DII and DIII schools, but when I got the phone call from the University of Minnesota - Moorhead that they gave their last scholarship to another player, it was on to UW-Stout. I absolutely loved it. Basketball, parties, friends who I actually felt like I had stuff in common with, girls... I even enjoyed some of my classes.

I redshirted my freshman year, played a few minutes a game my second year and went into my redshirt sophomore year with big expectations. I worked all summer long changing my shot and had turned into a pretty good shooter. How hard did I work? My nickname was "Gunner" because I was on "The Gun" so much. "The Gun" is an automatic rebounding machine that has a huge net that drops down under the basket, collects the rebounded shots and passes the ball back to you. Depending on what you shots you're working on you can get up around 500 in an hour. At the start of practice sophomore year I was slotted as the starting point guard, ahead of Blake Craft from Chicago, and Isaac Reece from Kansas. And, pretty quickly I went from starting to scout team — not because of my skill level — but because of my perfectionism. I had, as my coach called it, "analysis paralysis."

I had the same problem as Jeff Van Gundy, as he put it: "I was really good when I was doing individual workouts and playing against cones. No one could stop me, but those players were the ones who got in the way."

One turnover led to the next, and soon I wasn't even playing. I was crushed. Basketball was who I was as person. It's what I let define myself, and even though I worked so hard, I had failed. I was completely embarrassed. "You're so f$*%#*@ bad. You work harder than anyone on this team and you can't even get minutes."

What I did was the opposite of Arianna Huffington.

"If you don't internalize failure in a way that paralyzes you, it is very empowering. You say: 'Hey, I failed. But I'm here, and I'm healthy, and my children love me, and I have great friends. Life is ahead of me.' Suddenly, you're willing to take even bigger risks." — Arianna Huffington

A day before Christmas break my junior year I left a note on my coach's desk: "I stopped in to see you today, but need to let you know that I've decided it's time for me to step away from the game." I felt an unbelievable sense of relief.

I told everyone I was changing my major to History. Stout didn't offer it, which is why I was transferring and left the team. I transferred back home to the Junior College, UW-Wood County, and then to Loras College in Dubuque, IA the Fall of 2004. That lasted about 4 weeks as my mom called to let me know my grandpa was in the hospital and most likely wouldn't make it through the night. He had been battling cancer for the past 13 years. I went back to Marshfield, and after a week he was still alive. I'd already transferred schools, changed my major again (History to PhyEd after 2 weeks at Loras), so I decided to drop out of school. Yes, I was, at one point, a college dropout. Probably the only thing Kanye West and I have in common.

Chapter 3
DON'T PUT YOUR LIFE IN A BOX

I ended up going back to UW - Stout to just finish up school and get on with dreams of coaching college basketball. It was then that I started to learn what actually made me tick because it <u>wasn't</u> coaching DIII college basketball. Helping kids with passion and potential achieve their dreams is what made me "go."

When I started college, I thought I wanted to be a high school art teacher and coach basketball. Based on the recommendation of a friend, I took an Intro to Psychology class and found it a lot more intriguing than some hippie art teacher telling me how to hold my pencil in drawing class. And, because I ended up with an amazing advisor, Ed Biggerstaff, who truly understood the big picture, I majored in Psychology with a self-planned minor in Basketball Entrepreneurship. Yes, you read that right — Basketball Entrepreneurship. Things definitely can turn out a little differently than planned — and significantly better than planned — if you're willing to adapt, be aware of, and take advantage of opportunities.

- At 20, I wanted to be a high school teacher and coach high school basketball
- At 22, I wanted to coach college basketball
- At 24, I wanted to build a successful AAU program and

send players to high major DI schools from small towns in WI

- At 27, I decided to focus more on training, take a leap of faith and move to Milwaukee to start a training company and camps
- At 30, I decided I wanted to grow my business so eventually I can have someone else run it and try to get a job in the NBA or coaching college.
- At 31, I wanted to start a for-impact organization to work with inner-city, at-risk kids.

It may seem like it's crystal clear at the time, but you have to have the ability and willingness to adapt.

If your vision no longer fills you with passion, make a change. And, that's ok. Don't fight it. Embrace it. Spend time in thought. In the depths of your deepest thoughts you'll find something that sets your soul on fire.

I had to stop looking at it like I had failed. I hadn't failed. I could have went on to make a lot of money, helping kids, and doing something with meaning... but I didn't have the desire anymore. I still love being in the gym working with passionate players, but my heart was in DRIVE, the for-impact organization.

And to really figure this out for yourself, I think we all have to be a little selfish. Unless we are selfish — put ourselves first, and pursue things that we want — we can't give it away.

Jim Rohn says, "The more you become, the more you can give." This is so true. If we aren't selfish in pursuing who we want to be and what we want to accomplish, we can't give it away. We can't help others get what they want.

"Don't ask yourself what the world needs; ask yourself what makes you come alive. And then go and do that. Because what the world needs is people who have come alive." - Howard Thurman.

In order to do this, you have to be selfish. You have to do what you want so you can give what you become.

Chapter 4
HOW NOT TO GET HUNGOVER

When all we are focused on is success, especially if it's a very undefined picture, we set ourselves up for major expectation hangovers and disappointments. In high school, as a team, our coach would always have us write our goals at the beginning of the season and I'd put down the typical statistical things that we have come to define as success:

- 15PPG, 8APG and 5 Rebounds
- Conference Player of the Year
- All-Area
- All-State
- DI or DII Scholarship

In fact, I never accomplished any of these except All-Area. And, they were huge disappointments for me. Especially receiving that phone call from Minnesota State-Moorhead telling me that they had given their last scholarship to another kid (rightfully so).

The problem here is that we become so focused on a definition of success that actually is completely out of our control. Expectations are great, even required, as long as they are things we can control.

When we set expectations and goals that are outside of our control we set ourselves up for major disappointment.

An Expectation Hangover, defined by life coach and speaker, Christine Hassler, is this: the myriad of undesirable feelings, thoughts, and responses present when one or a combination of the following things occurs:

1. Things don't turn out the way you thought, planned or wanted them to.

2. Things do turn out according to your planned desires, but you don't feel the fulfillment you expected

3. You are unable to meet your personal and/or professional expectations

4. An undesired, unexpected event occurs that is in conflict with what you wanted or planned.

As you can see, I had some major hangovers. Why? Because everything I had set as an expectation as out of my control.

Should we dream? Absolutely. We have to have a vision to move us forward for us to evolve. It's human nature for you to want to strive for your potential. But, the things you need to do in order to reach this dream should always be within your control. And, you need to detach yourself from the results:

- How many sales calls am I going to make each day?
- How many shots am I going to make in my workout?
- How many books am I going to read per month?

These are all measurable commitments we have complete control over. When we make commitments we have control over, there isn't a chance for expectation hangovers or disappointment because they are all on us to complete. And, there isn't room for excuses because in the end, it all comes back to you

Chapter 5

WHY YOU SHOULDN'T WANT SUCCESS AS MUCH AS YOU WANT TO BREATHE

There is a popular YouTube video out there by Eric Thomas, or 'ET the Preacher' as he calls himself, that went viral a few years ago — especially in the sports world.

While I don't agree with everything in the video you should check it out for yourself if you haven't seen it. It's called "How Bad Do You Want It? (Success) HD."

The video is a voiceover of Eric Thomas with footage of a football player training in the weight room, on the beach and the field. He tells the story of a football player being trained by a guru who is supposed to lead him on his path to football greatness.

The first day they meet at the beach and the guru asks him: "How bad do you want to be successful?"

The football player responds, "real bad."

And the guru tells him to "walk out into the water."

So the player starts walking out into the water just up to his knees. The guru encourages him to keep walking, until the water is covering his waist, then shoulders, and eventually his head. When he gets that far the guru holds him down under the water until just before he passes out. He finally lets up as the football player gasps for air and says, "When you want to succeed as much as you want to breathe, then you'll be successful."

Is it inspirational? For sure. There are going to be times when you have to push yourself so hard that you feel like you are going to pass out.

Back when Kobe was on top of the NBA, Kevin Eastman, then Assistant Coach for the Celtics, ran into Kobe outside of the locker rooms prior to a game. Eastman asked Kobe, "What did you do for workouts last summer? You are having such a great year."

Kobe responded, " I didn't workout last summer"

A bit confused, Eastman asked him, "What do you mean you didn't workout? You're playing so well..."

To which Kobe said, "I didn't workout last summer. I had blackouts. I went so hard until I felt like I was going to blackout."

These were Kobe's Devil Workouts: 6 months per year, 6 days per week, 6 hours per day.

6AM-Martial Arts 1.5 hours
7:30-Track 1 hour
Weight Room: 1hr 15 minutes
Shooting and Skills: 3-4 hours
Therapy

Do you have to push yourself through fatigue, work on days you don't feel like it and make sacrifices most people would never even think of? Of course. But, the problem I have with this "want to succeed as much as you want to breathe" mindset is that it puts things that are uncontrollable as the focus of our efforts and attention. When you don't definite success for yourself it sets you up for major expectation hangovers.

Chapter 6

WHY YOU'RE NOT ACTUALLY CHASING SUCCESS

In the end, what we truly are searching for, is calmness. Peace of mind. Happiness. And not happiness in the sense that we desire things like money, clothes, and food. When we seek success in material things, once we get them, then what? It's like when you accomplish that huge goal you have, win the state championship, or get that college scholarship — yes it's great, but then what? Studies show that the happiness from accomplishing big goals actually only lasts a couple hours and in rare cases up to a month. When we seek things that are within us, not outside of us... these are lasting. Because these are things we become, not things we achieve. Is striving for things wrong? No, because it is in the striving, in the dreaming, in the struggles and challenges, that we become the person we need to be in order to seek the internal things. The calmness, the happiness, the peace of mind... knowing that you put forth your best effort in becoming the best you were able to become.

I have the same problem as Dan Harris, author of 10% Happier: "(Eckhart) Tolle was forcing me to confront the fact that the thing I'd always thought was my greatest asset—my internal cattle prod—was also perhaps my greatest liability."

"As part of my 'price of security' mind-set, I had long assumed that the only route to success was harsh self-criticism. However, research shows that 'firm but kind' is the smarter play. People trained in self-compassion meditation are more likely to quit smoking and stick to a diet. They are better able to bounce back from missteps. All successful people fail. If you can create an inner environment where your mistakes are forgiven and flaws are candidly confronted, your resilience expands exponentially." - Dan Harris

I am still learning this, reminding myself of this and working on it everyday. For years, I had attached my self-worth, calm, peace, and happiness to the level of players that we worked with. I really wanted to work the Nike Skills Academies. I kept telling myself that once I worked those events, with the best high school and college players in the country, that I would be validated. I would be the able to say to myself that I was one of the best in the country at teaching the game. Once we started working out more NBA players I would believe in myself and what our company was doing. But, the more I became mindful, the more I realized where the source of those desires came from. The need to feel validated. The need to feel like the work that I put so much time in to mattered. This is when I started to learn that you can't let anyone validate what you do. When you are really passionate about what you do it's really hard to draw the line between who you are and what you do. But, if you are looking for external validation you are always going to be looking for someone else to "let you into their club." If it was Nike, then it would be the NBA, if it was the NBA then it would be USA Basketball. Is it wrong to have these as dreams and strive for them? No, but you have to detach from them. You are not your dream. You are a human being. The effort you put forth, the way that you love others and yourself — that matters the most.

"What hurts a lot of people, particularly famous people, is they start valuing themselves for "what" they are, the way the world sees them: writer, speaker, basketball player. And you start believing that what you are is who you are. There's a big difference." — Kobe Bryant

The more I became mindful about WHY I really wanted to pursue certain things, the more I became aligned with things I truly wanted to pursue.

So I co-founded DRIVE, a non-profit that provides inner-city, at-risk youth access to professional basketball training, mentoring and personal development activities. Why? Because I realized that my dream really wasn't to work with NBA players. My dream, my purpose, my "why," was to help people who have big dreams achieve big dreams. To me, that was success.

And until you define it for yourself you will always be looking for something on the outside to fulfill yourself.

External Validation

In the basketball world, here is validation: the high school coach who wins the state championship, the college coach who wins the National Championship, or NBA coach who suddenly has a player with a breakout year.

I was sitting in the Syracuse Basketball office, talking to their assistant coaches, a quick stop on my way to Honesdale, PA, to work Five-Star. It was a year or two after they won the 2003 National Championship with Carmelo Anthony, and they had got bombarded with phone calls, emails, and speaking requests — everyone now wanted to learn their 2-3 Zone. Suddenly, Jim Boeheim was 10 times the coach he was. Overnight. Well, not really. The basketball world just validated his 2-3 Zone because they won the National Championship.

When Jeremy Lin sparked "Linsanity" with the New York Knicks, Kenny Atkinson, the Knicks Player Development Coach, suddenly was the best in the world at getting players better. Well, not really. He was always great — he just was validated.

When we start to let these external definitions of success define us, we lose focus on the thing that matters the most. The process.

We don't win games by focusing on winning. We win games by taking care of the basketball, playing great defense, and making all the little plays. We throw hand-to-hand passes, pivot under pressure, be there on the catch with greater shooters, always play the ball/see your man, and dive for every single 50/50 ball.

These are all things that are within our control.

Chapter 7

SHIFT #1: A RENEWED FOCUS ON READING

When I went back to school after my grandfather passed away, I took a Psychology class recommended by one of my friends. It was by far the most interesting class I had ever taken. Combine that with my personal struggle with depression, and I knew that's what I wanted to major in. This sparked a renewed interest in reading, which I had done a lot as a kid — I might have been the youngest kid ever to read Mitch Albom's <u>Fab Five</u> book.

I spend my last couple summers of college working basketball at Stout, for Forrest Larson, FutureStars, University of Minnesota, and Five-Star. I was around high school and college coaches all summer picking their brains. One question I started asking: suggestions on books to read.

Success is a Choice

I don't know who recommended it to me, but someone told me to read Rick Pitino's book, <u>Success is a Choice</u>. I will be forever indebted to them because it truly changed my life. Regardless of what you think of Pitino, the principles in the book are rock solid. I took to heart a chapter in the book called "Being Positive is a Discipline." It changed my life. It introduced the concept that being positive is a choice. It's not something that happens to us and not something we are born with. Holy Shit. He's right. Why didn't someone teach me this sooner?

Here's why this matters.

"Based on business consultant and psychologist, Marcial Losada's extensive mathematical modeling, 2.9013 to 1 is the ratio of positive to negative interactions necessary to make a corporate team successful. This means that it takes about three positive comments, experiences, or expressions to fend off the languishing effects of one negative. Dip below this tipping point, now known as the 'Losada Line,' and workplace performance quickly suffers. Rise above it, ideally, the research shows, to a ratio of 6 to 1 — and teams produce their very best work." Shawn Achor

Success is a Choice has since sparked a life-long journey of self-discovery, personal growth, developing awareness and mindfulness.

The Success Principles

The other book that really stuck with me was Jack Canfield's Success Principles, which said there are really only three things we can control in our lives:

1. Our thoughts
2. Feelings
3. Actions

The problem is that there are tens of thousands of books, videos, conferences, and speakers out there selling inspiration, motivation, and tools to try and help you reach your potential, get out of debt, be a better leader...you name it. There are even books on self-awareness. 99% of the things out there that people want to improve, someone has already done before.

"Success leaves footprints."

It might not be written in a way that resonates with you, it might be thousands of years old, like the Bible or Bhagavad Gita, but the path is there.

The problem is that none of these talk about the first step to improving anything — whether that's you, your organization, or team.

The first step is awareness.

How do you know what to get better at, if you don't know what you need to improve? Yes, there are things like evaluations to give you feedback. And those are extremely valuable. But they are valuable because they take the emotions out of everything and provide you with objective feedback. You might be spending your time on things that aren't in your area of highest contribution. Just because you are improving at something doesn't mean it's going to make the biggest impact.

How do you know what's going to make the biggest impact without awareness? Being truly aware of your environment, organization, and the people you serve.

From ages 22-31, I read quite a bit. Probably around 250-300 books. I haven't kept track, but 95% of them were because I wanted to improve fix this pain, improve myself or our business. The other 5% we won't talk about, but I did read <u>Eat, Pray, Love.</u> It's actually a really good book (if you haven't read it).

Reading did a lot of things, but the biggest impact it had was it helped me change my mindset. It helped me realize I had a choice in every single situation I was in. And, even though I might have limited options, there was always a choice.

I realized the choices I was making every single second, of every minute of every hour of every day, week, and year were going to add up. It's the small choices you make now that lead up to the big wins in the future.

Chapter 8

SHIFT #2: CONTROLLING WHAT YOU CAN CONTROL

Until we create more awareness in our lives, it's hard to conceptualize all the things that are truly out of our control. And, all the time and energy we waste try to control these things? When you break it down there are really only three things in your life that you can control.

Thoughts, feelings, and actions.

Our thoughts are processed in our mind as images because this is how we give meaning to them. Before written word and language, we learned by observing others doing things.

In fact, recent research shows that our expectations create brain patterns that can be just as real as those created by events in the real world. That's pretty powerful stuff. So whether we are worried about something in the future or visualizing something positive, our brain is creating these patterns that affect how we feel.

Unfortunately, too many people waste so much energy on things they cannot control. The end result is that when it comes to the things they can control they are absolutely exhausted. They expend so much trying to change the uncontrollable instead of focusing on what's next and what they can learn.

When Steve Nash was playing at Santa Clara as a freshman, he was getting the ball stolen from him up almost every possession. Instead of getting emotional, upset or losing his confidence he simply went to his defender and asked, "Why is it so easy to steal the ball from me?" He was able to take that feedback, make changes to his technique and stop turning the ball over. We always have a choice, but we're not always aware of the choice.

AWARENESS

Being aware of what you can and cannot control is an unbelievably empowering skill. Yes, it's a skill. In fact, it is critical to reaching your potential. I never knew I had it until I found the ability to be aware.

I ask this question during camps and speeches. If you get an F on test, don't get hired for a job, or get absolutely hammered driving to the basket, but the ref doesn't call a foul, do you automatically get mad or upset? Almost all the hands go up.

Then I ask – if you see someone else get an F on a test, not hired for a job, or get absolutely hammered on a drive to a basket without a foul called, do they automatically get mad or upset?

Some kids will answer: "No they can decide what they want to do."

Sometimes we don't see things clearly until look outside ourselves — when we create separation between stimulus and response. And that's what mindfulness

gives us the power to do.

You have a choice. You can get mad, or you can move on to the next thing. It's simple, but it's not obvious. Remember: the most profound thoughts are simple and even those might not be easy. You always have a choice.

YOUR THOUGHTS

Your thoughts influence every thing you do. It is crazy how many thoughts will go through your mind throughout the day. Think about the 4 people who really influence your life:
1. Parents
2. Friends
3. Coaches/Bosses/Co-Workers
4. Teachers

Your parents might say 10 things to you during a day, even though you will never know the influence of them.

Your friends might say 20 things to you during the course of a day. These things determine what kind of music you listen to, how you dress, how you treat your teachers to seem cool, and how you treat others throughout the day.

Your coach or boss might say 5 things to you. 2 positive and 3 "constructive criticism." And based on all the coaches I've had, that's probably exaggerating.

How many thoughts do you have going through your head during practice or workday? Research says it's in the thousands — over 50,000 in an 8-hour work or school day.

"Man, I'm good!" after you make a great play or get an A on a test.

"Don't turn the ball over. Don't turn the ball over." With someone pressuring you on defense.

"I can't shoot!" after you miss 2 shots in a row

"This proposal isn't good enough. I have to change it or I'm going to be a failure."

So during a workday or practice, thousands of thoughts might go through your head, but your coach or boss only says five.

What you think about, matters. Tremendously. Why? Because our thoughts are processed as images; the images tell ourselves a story, and the story we tell ourselves — the emotions we attach to those stories — affect how we feel.

If you are someone really striving to be the best, I'd be willing to bet the average of your thoughts (positive thoughts + negative thoughts) is a very accurate representation of how you feel about yourself.

A challenge with this is defining what a positive and negative thought is. Contrary to popular belief, it can't be things like, "Don't worry about it. You'll get it next time." While that's not necessarily wrong, it's not the most helpful. A positive thought is something that is BOTH truthful and beneficial, like "You're better than that.

Keep your weight forward and toes turned on your shot" Many times we'll realize that what we are telling ourselves, over and over again, is nothing close to the truth.

When we start to be more mindful, we can detach from our thoughts, look at them objectively, and perceive reality more accurately. Until we become aware of our thoughts, we are letting our unconscious mind significantly impact our actions. Changing our mindset is first about being able to bring our unconscious to the conscious.

The most important conversation you will ever have is the one you will have with yourself. Think about it — would you ever talk to a friend the way that you talk to yourself?

YOUR FEELINGS

If the other team blatantly fouls one of your players in a game you absolutely have a choice how you respond. Do you let your emotions impact your decision-making on the next play? The only thing you can control?

If your boss gives you some constructive criticism, do you choose how you feel? Do you see the feedback as an opportunity to grow, or as an attack on you as a person?

It's your choice.

If your significant other breaks up with you, can you choose how you feel?

When I was in 9th grade, this girl broke up with me. I was

devastated. Crushed. I let her determine how I feel, how I acted, and what I did. For months. You know what she is doing now with her life? I have no idea. My point is, I let her decide how I felt for months of my life. That's a long time to be unhappy. Did she really decide?

No. I did!

It is work to choose and try to make yourself feel great. As the one of America's foremost business philosopher, Jim Rohn said, "Happiness is not an accident – nor is it something you wish for. It's something you design."

If you lose a close game you have a choice how you respond. You have a choice how you feel after the game. I used to think the people who showed a ton of emotion and cried after the game were the only people who really cared. Not true at all. The less you are on an emotional rollercoaster the better your ability to respond in an even-keel manner. It's a big part of what makes Kobe such an incredible performer. He's never too high, and never too low. When he hits a game-winning shot, he acts like he's been there before, thousands of times.

ACTIONS

To further compound your thoughts and feelings, the ability to choose your actions is one of the most powerful things in the world that no one can ever take away from you. Yes, there are things that happen every day that you cannot control, but you have a choice in how you respond. If something negative happens, that doesn't mean you have to respond in a negative way. No matter how your day starts: if you run out of toothpaste, miss the bus, or have someone close to you pass away... You have the power to respond positively.

It's about having a growth mindset.

And, instead of asking "Why me?" You start to ask, "What can I learn?"

Your actions are a result of your feelings. Most people act upon what they feel.

If you are aware of your thoughts, you can choose how you feel, therefore influencing your actions. By being aware of negative thoughts, you can notice patterns on how it affects your actions.

You have a choice no matter what situation you are in. You may not like the consequences or the byproduct of your options, but you always have a choice.

The better choices you make today the better your options in the future will become.

You need to believe that you choose your own destiny.

"Until you make the unconscious conscious, it will direct your life and you will call it fate." – Carl Jung

Every minute of every day you have choice that you can make that determine your future. They determine your tomorrow, next week, next month. After consecutive correct choices you can start to build on success. No one makes you feel or do anything. You always have a choice.

Your thoughts influence how you feel.

How you feel influences how you act.

Your actions become habits.

And, your habits ultimately determine who you become and what you accomplish.

You literally do become your thoughts.

Chapter 9

SHIFT #3: THE PURSUIT OF HAPPINESS MYTH

By age 31 I had developed a pretty successful business, and like growing up, by all external definitions should have been happy. But, I also entered the most stressful time of my adult life. Trying to continue to grow our business, start up DRIVE, along with an unhealthy relationship. I was stressed. Maybe that's an understatement. I don't know how to describe it except the way I did to a therapist, " I literally feel like I am dying inside."

And it took me a while to realize that if you're a motivated person, really wanting to make an impact on the world, there is always going to be something more. But the key is to do the work, and let go of the outcome.

Easy to say.

Hard as hell to do.

Things were moving way too fast. The kids we started working with in 7th grade were playing in the NCAA tournament and my dog was almost 4 years old in the blink of an eye. The days were long, but the years were short.

The mistake I made was that I kept telling myself, "Just

make some money from this next project and you can go on vacation for a week" (I didn't take a vacation for the first 5 years out of college, and even then, my first one was 4 days).

What I didn't realize is that unless you're really selfish with yourself — you don't truly love yourself with your entire heart — you can't make the impact you dream about.

Here is my favorite poem on love written by my Breathwork Teacher:

"I am in this body but I am not the body. I and the body are separate. The body is mine for only a short time. Even if I live a hundred years more, it will go by like a flash. Everything outside of my heart is not truly mine. I own nothing in this world. Everything I own is contained in my heart. The love I have for others and the love they feel for me is mine. My connection with God is mine. My wisdom is mine. My joy is mine. I breathe into my heart-and breathe out from my heart. May I not waste another moment withholding love." - John Paul Crimi

Being a life-long learner, I got into a habit around this time of listening to podcasts at night before I went to bed. One of my favorites is "The Good Life Project" with Jonathon Fields; he had a guest on talking about the benefits of yoga. Not just for your body, but mainly for your mind. I'd done yoga in the past in college and off and on at the health clubs, but I'd always seen it as a physical practice. A practice for stretching, injury prevention, and a little bit of core work. The yoga they were talking about was 'Hot Vinyasa Yoga' where you practice in anywhere from 95-105 degree heat. He also talked about the harm of stress on your body and the toxins that can just drain your energy. Because in 'hot yoga' you sweat so much, and there is an emphasis on your breath, it helps flush out harmful toxins. The other part that intrigued me was how it can calm your mind, slow your brain activity, and help you feel more relaxed.

Even though it was 10 degrees outside in Milwaukee that January I looked up a place called Milwaukee Power Yoga, and gave it a try. After one class with Erin Highland, I was addicted, even though I couldn't do half of the poses. The more I practiced, the less I was stressed. And, because of this calmness I felt so much more aware of my feelings and environment. Yes, I'm talking about "feelings." That ever-so-dreaded word in the sports world.

I hated it, but I was talking about it. The truth is, every single action we take is to make us feel something... mainly to make us happy and feel safe enough to survive. I know that sounds kind of "new agey" but when you really break it down, and continually ask yourself "why," it really comes down to those two things.

Every action we take, consciously or subconsciously, is to make us happy. The clothes we wear, food we eat, and people we surround ourselves with, are all done to make us happy. Though, when we really think about it, all those things are out of control. We are assuming people will like our clothes, the food will taste good, and those people will elevate our lives.

But, when we can see happiness as something internal, something we choose and work towards. And, not something we hope for, we give ourselves a much better chance at achieving this.

"If you work with your mind, you will alleviate all the suffering that seems to come from the outside." - Pema Chodron

"The pursuit of happiness becomes the source of our unhappiness" - Dan Harris

Don't believe me? This is verbatim, a conversation I had with an NCAA DI basketball player:

ML: Why do you want to start on your team?

Player: Because it's been a dream of mine.

ML: Why has it been a dream?

Player: Because I enjoyed playing.

ML: Why'd you enjoy playing the game?

Player: Because it made me happy.

ML: Why did it make you happy?

Player: Because it validated that I was good at something?

ML: Why did you need to feel validated that you were good at something?

Player: To make myself feel needed, safe and secure.

When we get to the root of it, that is the answer for everyone. Crazy, but true.

DEVELOPING COMPASSION

The more I practiced Yoga the more I saw myself become aware of my thoughts, aware of how I treated others, and became more compassionate.

And as I continued to practice, the more I became aware of my feelings and thoughts. This gives you the insight to why you do things and why others do things.

"Out of this insight, compassion is born" - Pema Chodron

I also started to see the relationship between mindfulness and what every athlete reading this book has experienced — being in the zone. That experience where everything just flows...you are completely immersed in the moment...only relying upon your habits.

The more I practiced yoga, the easier it was for me to be present, which is exactly the state we want to be in when we are playing the game, coaching, or working on a big project. In many ways, especially when we are first starting out, yoga is a type of moving meditation. You are so focused on the poses that you have to be present. I can't tell you how many times I have fallen out of a balancing pose only to immediately notice that my mind was somewhere else. For me, like a lot of others, it was the gateway to meditation.

Chapter 10
SHIFT #4: MEDITATING LIKE A BUDDHIST

My meditation journey started on 'The Art of Charm' podcast I heard about a guided meditation iPhone app called "Headspace." They had a free trial to get you started called "Take 10," which were ten, 10-minute guided meditation sessions. Mindfulness meditation is a practice, so, just like learning a new skill, we need a teacher.

But, before we begin, let's get one thing clear. This book is NOT about trying to impose a new belief system or religion. I'm not trying to convince you to go live in the mountains or join a Buddhist Monastery. It is completely secular.

Meditation is training your mind for life. It's training your mind to be comfortable in uncomfortable situations.

Every single coach in America agrees that a percentage of sports is mental. But how much time do you actually spend working on it? I guarantee you spend more time on the court and in the weight room than intentionally training your brain. Yes, there absolutely are situations during practice and games where we are teaching a mentality, but it's not intentional and focused on a specific mental aspect like playing in pressure situations.

When I started, honestly, it was so hard to justify spending time doing it. And usually, the only time I did it was when I was going through something stressful with work or a relationship. I'd take get my headphones out, load the app and "Take 10." And, sometimes "Take 30" depending how stressed I was. The problem was that I was doing this as a reaction to whatever was happening in my life. Instead, I should have been proactive, preventing this stress and anxiety from coming up, through daily practice.

New research is showing that daily meditation literally can physically change the makeup of the brain. The part of your brain responsible for the flight or flight response, your amygdala (Yes the funny name Adam Sandler jokes about in "Waterboy"), starts to calm down and become less reactive.

Daily practice has also made me more aware of when any anxiety or stress was coming on. Something I think everyone deals with, but isn't aware of, or just flat out denies. Most people don't know how calm and relaxed they are actually supposed to feel.

Many times, these thoughts, anxieties, or stresses are not rooted in reality. They are not proportionate to what is actually happening. Once we are able to become aware of our thoughts and detach from them we realize what we are telling ourselves is usually nothing close to the truth.

And, let's get one thing clear. A state of inner peace, calm and relaxation is not about being soft. I have fought this for years and still do today. Even if I'm ridiculously sore from a summer of camps,

I feel guilty getting a massage. It's about taking care of yourself so you have the love and energy to give to the rest of the world.

"Simply put, meditation for stress soothes our nervous system. While stress activates the 'fight or flight' part of our nervous system, mindfulness meditation activates the 'rest and digest' part of our nervous system, helping with stress management. Our heart rate slows, our respiration slows and our blood pressure drops. This is often called the 'relaxation response.' While chronic activation of the fight or flight response can be extremely damaging to the body, the relaxation response is restorative, so meditation benefits our wellbeing." - Headspace.com

Until you really start to internalize the statement below, daily practice might seem like a waste of time. You'll always be thinking that there are other things you could be doing. (Trust me.)

Meditation doesn't take time. It gives time.

What?

That doesn't make sense at all. You're obviously taking time to sit when you practice meditation everyday, but let's explore.

Mahatma Gandhi, who was a ridiculously busy leader, trying to drive a colonial power out of his homeland, and keep Hindus and Muslims from slaughtering one another, once said, "I have so much to accomplish today that I must meditate for two hours instead of one."

Why? Because he knew that it would allow him to access a

deeper state of flow, focus and productivity.

It's not sitting in a zombie-like state and just staring at something or sitting with your eyes shut. It's actually the opposite — it's becoming completely aware of your senses. Look at it this way. If you can't sit and just be aware of your thoughts and focus on your breath, how can you expect yourself to do this in pressure situations? How are you supposed to get into a state of flow shooting free throws down by 1 with 4 seconds left, or trying to draw up a set for your team with 9 seconds on the clock, or making a crucial decision that will affect your organization?

Like all training, it's going to be frustrating, and it's going to be work. When you are sitting, no matter if you've been doing it for a year, or it's your first time, you are going to have thoughts arise. The goal is not the get rid of your thoughts. The goal is to be aware of them and detach from them.

And, the ultimate goal is to drop the goal. To be completely present.

But when first starting out, the goal is to just see them as thoughts. You don't need to act on them. You don't need to attach meaning to them. You don't need to let them snowball into anxiety, fear, or even depression.

Your goal is to become the watcher. You are not your thoughts. You are the observer of your thoughts. You and your

thoughts are not the same.

And when we become the watcher we begin to experience things on a completely new level. There is a huge difference between <u>doing</u> things and <u>experiencing</u> things. Many people <u>do</u> a lot of things, they have a lot of toys, and attend events. But you're not truly living until you can start to <u>experience</u> everything. And, you can't be productive — focusing on the process — unless you are completely lost in the task at hand.

Here is an example of what goes through my head when I sit each day. And yes I mean every day. Not just when I first started:

Focus on your breath. 1 with the inhale. 2 with the exhale. 3...Allen Iverson wore number 3. Man that dude was so fun to watch. He changed the game. Iverson crossover? I remember working on that all the time before my freshman year in high school. I should have worked harder in high school. I wonder what Justin Matsick is doing (friend from high school). He needs to come visit me in LA. Man, it's beautiful here. But I get distracted. How can I work hard when I'm here. But what's the point of life? To just work hard all the time. Geez, this whole thing is a waste of time. I need to get stuff done. Wait, what breath am I on...

The longer you practice the longer the gaps will become between your thoughts. The moments when you are completely present. And, the more you practice the more you will have these moments throughout your day.

If we can first start by just focusing on our breath, letting thoughts come and go—and not attaching to them emotionally — we can begin to detach from them when they occur throughout our day and throughout practice. By detaching it allows us to have greater clarity. We see things for what they are, not what our past experiences tell us they are. And, as we'll see later, these stories we tell ourselves are one of the biggest predictors of success and happiness.

BOOK II
COME WITH ME

Chapter 11
PERFECT AWARENESS

Mindfulness is a buzz word that can mean many different things to many people, but for the purpose of this book, let's define it as simply being more aware.

Awareness is key. If we aren't aware, we can't make changes. If we don't change we can't improve. Awareness is key.

"When the mind disappears and thoughts disappear, you become mindful. What is mindfulness? It is awareness. Perfect awareness." - Osho

"Mindfulness means paying attention in a particular way: on purpose, in the present moment, and nonjudgmentally" - Jon Kabat-Zinn

Before I even heard the word mindfulness, I was really trying to be more "aware" of everything around me — especially my thoughts. The challenge? I didn't have a specific tool to do this. It's like trying to improve your jumper or golf swing with absolutely zero instruction.

I had read hundreds of books on personal development, leadership, and management. And, in each one of those I learned something, or it reinforced something, that I believed was a key to success. Something to make you work harder, work smarter, communicate better, work more consistently, be a better leader, a better decision maker, a better entrepreneur, a better speaker, a better writer, more vulnerable, a better coach, or a better connector. You name it, I read about it.

"Intelligence is the door to freedom and alert attention is the mother of intelligence." - Jon Kabat-Zinn

I agree that each one of these principles is crucial to becoming who you want to be and becoming the best you can at what you want to do. Alone these success principles will help you bridge the gap. But, as I'll explain soon, mindfulness meditation will significantly amplify each of these principles.

The great thing about it is that you don't have to do them individually. You don't have to, even though you can, meditate on things like being a better leader. If you are simply being more mindful in everything you do, you are going to enhance all of the success principles. Leadership, discipline, communication, and intentional effort — all of these will be significantly enhanced through meditation.

Meditation can take on a lot of different meanings. It's a vague term that can be used to describe several different types of meditations like visualization, stress reduction meditation, transcendental, and mantra-based meditations.

It's to create more awareness of your thoughts, feelings and actions so you can be more intentional about how you spend your time, and find inner peace in everything you do.

"To find our way, we will need to pay more attention to this moment. It is the only time that we have in which to live, grow, feel, and change." - Jon Kabat-Zinn

Kobe Bryant, Michael Jordan, Oprah Winfrey, Steve Jobs, Paul McCartney, John Lennon, Russell Simmons, Lebron James, Phil Jackson... I'm sure you've guessed it by now. They all meditate(d). Daily.

"Until you make the unconscious conscious, it will direct your life and you will call it fate." - Carl Jung

For purposes of focus and productivity mindfulness meditation familiarizes people with that ever-elusive state of flow. The one where we are in the zone. See, being present and being in the flow share extremely similar qualities. When we can tap into it through meditation is helps us carry out that state of mind into the rest of our day.

The true freedom gained from this practice is not a withdrawal from life or repressing emotions — it's to be more consciously engaged in all of your life.

So how can Mindfulness Meditation amplify each one of these principles?

Let's explore.

Chapter 12
THE POWER OF A VISION

I truly believe that having a vision for yourself is the first step to achieving success —your definition of success. Some people say the first thing you need is a work ethic, but if you don't have a clear vision you don't know what you're working towards. It all goes back to mindfulness and being completely aware of your thoughts and feelings. We don't chase things because of what they are. We aren't chasing that scholarship, state championship or more money because of the goal itself.

We chase things, we dream about things because of the meaning we attach to them and the way they will make us feel when we earn them.

This is completely different from goal setting, which I'm not even a fan of. Why? Because almost all goals are completely outside your control. Create your vision based on things you can control and the feeling you're trying to achieve.

I co-founded DRIVE because I knew nothing else in my professional life made me feel better than helping kids with big dreams achieve big dreams. Especially kids with so much stacked against them...with so much guilt, shame, and negativity in their life. To know I had a part in getting them access to opportunities they couldn't get anywhere else, helping them develop a vision and providing hope. That is what made me feel on top of the world.

If you are not aware of your thoughts and feelings, how can you expect yourself to have an authentic vision that aligns with what your heart wants?

It is the fundamental building block of your journey. In any type of adversity, a person, business, teacher, or athlete will always revert to their fundamentals in times of distress. What vision or belief are you truly committed to and rooted in? This is what is going to keep you going when you think you can go no more.

"It's the effort after you've given your all that matters the most." - Unknown

What do you want to be when you grow up? Seriously. What would you be if there was no chance you could fail? You can't listen to the people who tell you that you can't or shouldn't. The only reason they tell you that you can't is because they are jealous of your talents and abilities or don't want to put forth the effort that you are willing to.

Parents might tell you "No" because they don't want you to hurt from a potential failure.

But that's only because they view failure and struggle as permanent — not part of the growth process.

Maybe they don't know how to dream, or know that the most successful people in the world started everything with a dream, and vision, for where they want to take their life.

Visiting Santa Monica, CA, in September 2013, I got an unwavering sense of "home" — a sense of peace, of calm I hadn't experienced before — and decided this was where I wanted to eventually live. I took several pictures from Palisades Park which overlooks Santa Monica beach and out to the Pacific Ocean. These became my desktop screensaver and iPad lock screen — the two things I saw to start my day and end my night. I visualized myself there in the mornings, taking Peyton (my dog) for walks and starting my day being grateful for what I had — setting the tone for the rest of the day to pursue the things I wanted, and who I wanted to become.

About a year later, I decided to move, and when I arrived in late November, I ended up living at a place five blocks from the exact spot that I took that picture. On my first night there — after about two hours after arriving, I took Peyton for a walk down to that same spot I took the picture. It was so relaxing and surreal... actually doing the same thing I had visualized when I visited there a year before.

When you vividly and consistently

visualize something, you are subconsciously making actions that will get you to that vision.

People persist through adversity only when they have a vision — **one they are emotionally connected to.** As the leader of your basketball program, business, or school, it's your responsibility to ignite the vision with input from the people you're leading . What does every player in your program work for and dream of? If it's winning a conference championship each year, what does that feel like? What is the environment like? What does it sound like? What reputation or brand do you want your family to have?

If I'm a basketball coach, I'm creating a vision based on a collective team effort — the most significant is a defensive stop. If I'm a leader of an organization I'm creating a vision where the client or stakeholder is the hero — we are there to assist them along the way to achieve their dreams.

Read This If You're A Coach:

"It's March... and your team is playing at home, against your rival, for the conference championship... you and your team walk out on the floor for warm-ups and the gym is packed. Standing room only. There are students, parents, and community members there with signs made, faces painted, and everyone is wearing your school colors. Fast forward to the 4th quarter with 23 seconds left, your team is on defense in the half-court with a 1-point lead. The opposing team starts their offense, but your on ball defense is perfection — bothering without fouling. The closeouts are text book — high hands, containing the drive, until one player gets beat, but like you practiced all year, the helpside is there and on the kick out the rotational defender "helps the helper" as the game clock expires. They don't even get a shot off. The gym goes crazy and you can't even hear yourself. That's why you emphasized the details, fought through fatigue in practice and sacrificed all year long. Some of that wasn't fun, but this is. THIS is fun."

Read This If You Are A Player:

"It's the conference championship being played at your school.

You run out for warm ups, the gym is packed with fans wearing your school's colors, their faces painted and signs made. The band is playing, the place is buzzing and it's standing room only — 20 minutes before tipoff.

Fast forward to the 4th quarter.

Your team has the ball down by 1 with 11 seconds left.

Your coach calls a timeout, draws up an isolation play to put the ball in your hands and says, "Go win us the conference championship."

The ball is inbounded to you at the top of the key, calmly wait for the inbound to get in to position. With 8 seconds left you put the ball on the floor to get into your rhythm, cross the ball over, get cut off, change again and get to the rim, finish with the "Go-To" move you ceaselessly worked on all off-season. The packed gym goes crazy. It's so loud you can't hear yourself."

That's why you need a vision. And being mindful helps you

uncover a vision that aligns with your truest, most authentic self.

Chapter 13
THE 4 STEP PROGRAM

1. You must start with a vision

2. Get an accountability or workout partner

3. Workout/work to music

4. Write out your workout or schedule your work. What gets scheduled gets done.

Let's explore.

1.   You Must Have A Vision. And, the clearer the vision, the clearer your thoughts the better your focus. What is going to get you through the ball handling drills when your forearms burn? What's going to make you do that last set of squats when your legs feel like jello?

You aren't "training" or working unless you are intentionally, effectively and efficiently practicing a skill. No matter what that skill is. You have to be doing all three of those things. Training them until they become habits.

"In high pressure situations you won't rise to the occasion. You'll default to your level of training" - Navy SEALS

That's why you need a vision.

2.   Get A Notebook. It doesn't have to be anything more than a spiral notebook you use for science or math class. Use this notebook to write down new drills, moves or teaching points you learn from workouts, camps or watching games. The second use of this notebook is to write out your workouts in a detailed and organized fashion before you get to the gym. If I were you, I'd write them out before I go to bed each night. Write out exactly what you are going to do and how many reps you are going to perform for each drill. By writing out your workouts it's like making a contract with yourself and you are much more likely to do the workout when you get to the gym. This will also be something you can look back on to give you confidence when things might not be going that great for you. If you have a bad shooting game you can look back on that notebook and see that you shot 15,000 shots over the last 4 months. It was just a bad night.

Sometimes you need to look back on all that you have done instead of always looking forward to the future. You might not believe me, but there are definitely times when I think to myself, "Man, what am doing? Are you actually helping people? Are you actually making an impact and helping people achieve their dreams?" When I get in these mindsets a couple things I do are look back on the testimonials that people have given me in the past. There is no way that NBA players like Steph Curry, and coaches like Dee Brown and NCAA DI coaches like Buzz Williams are going to put their name on the line for someone who isn't doing a great job teaching the game and making an impact. Sometimes I get caught up in my own mind games. My own trouble perceiving what is truly reality. And, yes, as an organization we are making an impact. The guys who work for us are some of the most passionate, caring, selfless people I have ever met. They impact lives daily. And, I have to look back and know that I've provided them with a platform to do this.

The notebook is a source of confidence.

3.   **Get A Workout Or Accountability Partner.** Simply put – shooting alone sucks. And, chasing a vision is tough to do alone. Having an accountability partner does three things:

Accountability: find someone who is going to push you and hold you accountable on days that you don't want to workout. Someone who shares common goals and dreams with you. You will become the average of the 5 people that your surround yourself with the most. Choose wisely.

Rebounder: It gives you someone you can do game like shooting drills with. Game shots from game spots at game speed. If you're not alone in the gym chasing the ball you're going to enjoy working on your shot a lot more.

1-on-1: Playing 1-on-1 is one of the best things you can do to work on your game in the off-season as long as you are doing it the right way. It also helps fuel that competitive fire.

4.   **Listen To Music.** Use music during your workouts as a source of energy and enthusiasm. Your workouts will be much more intense. Research states that music actually does have a physiological affect on our energy levels and focus.

"The right music can make a bad workout into a stellar sweat session. Don't just take our word for it, science agrees." A recent study from the Kellogg School of Management at Northwestern University revealed that music has the ability to push us to do our best, especially tunes with heavy bass. If you think about it, it's a pretty easy way efficiently and effectively to increase your productivity.

Chapter 14
COMPASSION IS TOUGHNESS

Developing compassion is a key trait of great leaders. It's not about being soft. It's about making sure the people you are leading know you genuinely care about them. It's about breaking down barriers, and being vulnerable.

Your ability to influence is directly related to your willingness to be vulnerable.

It's so cliché and it's so true. People don't care what you know until they know how much you care.

"Now, 'compassion' is not a word often bandied about in locker rooms. But I've found that a few kind, thoughtful words can have a strong transformative effect on relationships, even with the toughest men in the room." - Phil Jackson

Compassion breaks down barriers among people. You have to develop the ability to feel what they feel. When we feel what someone else feels we have a much better understanding of what they need. And, a much clearer understanding of how we can help them and serve them.

Awareness gives us the ability to have compassion, empathy, and serve others. It gives us the ability to walk in their shoes. When someone is being rude or disrespectful to you, you have no idea what happened to him or her that day. It increases empathy.

They might not be as lucky as you to have had the support system or access to education that you did, which enables you to stay calm in those situations. To respond in a healthy manner and not react.

Taking the subway, traveling in an airplane or riding the bus can be beautiful because it puts you in an oddly intimate setting with people from all different walks of life. Basketball is similar. My brother played AAU with the Running Rebels, an inner-city Milwaukee-based program and it forced everyone in my family into what was then an uncomfortable situation. Uncomfortable, not because of the actual situation. Uncomfortable because of the perception of the situation. Growing up in a small town in central Wisconsin, the only thing you know about the inner-city and black community is through rap music, MTV, the news, and basketball. As naive as that may sound, it's the truth. It's the perception. On top of that, Milwaukee is <u>extremely</u> segregated compared to other metropolitan areas in the country. So you have these people from small-town central Wisconsin, developing relationships, being teammates, and allowing their son to be coached by people who have completely different stories and experiences.

If we don't develop compassion, we miss out on so many opportunities — opportunities to serve, to grow, to learn, and to see the good in all of these experiences.

Chapter 15
CONNECT. INVEST. INFLUENCE.

Communication is one of the hardest things I've had to learn both personally and professionally. It's a challenge for me because to do it authentically you have to be extremely vulnerable — something I think everyone struggles with.

One thing I've learned is you have to communicate different ways to different people. When I first started coaching I tried to address everyone at the same time with the same message. While that is okay to do with very general expectations, I found it was much more effective to connect with the players individually on their level.

It's not about what you understand — it's about what they understand.

Connecting individually might be more effort upfront, but it's a much better way to make sure there is clarity in your message and expectations.

Your players, students, or even employees all have unique experiences that have led them to this point in their life. No one has the same story as theirs. And, you can't communicate with them like they do.

Does a kid come from a home where his parents have really high expectations — maybe even unrealistic — and are really hard on him? You can't yell at that kid. He's already getting more of that at home than he needs. It's counter productive. This is a kid who needs to be reminded about the fun involved in the game and why he started playing in the first place. He might even be a kid, dare I say, who you joke around with during practice. If you want better performance you have to add in the element of fun. Why? Because it helps you achieve that state of flow. You can't have anxiety and feel pressure at the same time you're in the zone.

If a kid comes from a single parent home, where he doesn't have much supervision and is responsible for a lot of things on his own, you probably need to challenge the kid more. Kids like that need structure and accountability. They might even crave it because it gives them a sense of security.

Mindfulness gives you the ability to be more aware of where your players are coming from in order to connect with them in a deeper, more meaningful way.

"Connecting is the ability to identify with people and relate to them in a way that increases your influence with them." - John Maxwell

If you really want to connect in a meeting — because each player, student, or employee is different — you need to take the time to prepare. It doesn't have to be an hour-long research process, even though, depending on who it is, that might really pay off. Take a few minutes beforehand to just write out a couple questions. This will show them that you are sincere in your efforts to be there for them. To serve them.

Making compliments is a part of serving others that is often overlooked. When giving compliments, are they generic like "good job," or are they sincere and specific? Research shows people receive sincere and specific compliments better. Here's what I mean.

When someone finishes (makes a layup) through contact, do you say:

"Great job Billy!"

or

"Great job putting your inside shoulder on your defender, initiating the contact and taking them out of the play."

I used to work basketball camps all summer long for a coach named Forrest Larson, who runs his 'Take It To The Rim Skills Camps' in the Midwest. My main job was to be the demonstrator for the skills, drills, and concepts that he was teaching. I specifically remember a few times where I'd demonstrate a move or was running a station where he would specifically compliment me on something. I still remember these 10+ years later.

He would say, "I really like how you added this (part) to the drill. That's really good stuff."

If you're in a position of influence like a teacher or coach you're expected to constantly give feedback. That's how the people you're leading make changes and ultimately improve. But there's a trap you can fall into if you're not mindful. You have to ask yourself, "Am I communicating out of reaction and habits, or am I communicating intentionally?

Are you the coach that screams,"Come On!!!! You gotta execute!"?

"When you connect with others, you position yourself to make the most of your skills and talents." - John Maxwell

Kevin Eastman, VP of Basketball Operations for the Los Angeles Clippers, has an awesome rule about connecting with people. Whenever he meets someone new he doesn't ask for anything for a MINIMUM of the first year that he knows him or her. He finds ways to continually provide value to that person by sending them books or articles he thinks will resonate with them.

John Maxwell says there are three questions everyone asks, consciously or subconsciously, when first meeting someone.

1) Do you care for me?

2) Can you help me?

3) Can I trust you?

Like Eastman, truly INVESTING in the relationship adds value the other person, and to your relationship. This is the best way to connect.

Chapter 16

LIVE BY YOUR PRINCIPLES. NOT YOUR FEELINGS.

Being an entrepreneur isn't all it's cracked up to be. Yes there are the perks – you don't have to wait until the clock strives 5 to take that run outside if you so choose. But being the sole "boss" involves discipline, accountability and great responsibility. If you don't put in the work, you don't succeed. Being an entrepreneur can be both a gift and curse.

Unfortunately, I was getting into a bad pattern and experiencing more of the curse. If I didn't feel like doing the work, which happened often, I would put it off until the last minute. I let my feelings dictate my actions. The more I did this, the easier it was to put stuff off.

Yet, with my paralyzing anxiety also came guilt for not getting work done that day, or worse, shame and I'd just crawl back under the covers. I couldn't count the days I couldn't get out of bed.... days where if you told me, "Kobe Bryant is coming to the gym today and wants to get a workout in," I would said, "I don't care." All I wanted to do was sleep away the pain, the guilt, the shame. True, at times I was I tired or needed a break. But mostly I was depressed.

To combat this pattern, and the depression, I would work all weekend, or stay up working until 2 a.m. Of course, none of this was sustainable and negatively impacted my life.

The Impact of Mindfulness

Fortunately, with the help of mindfulness, I began to realize the underlying problem: I was spending significant time based on how I felt, *not* according to my values. Great coaches, leaders and parents lead from their values. Great players don't wake up at 6 a.m. jacked up to go work out. It's a conscious decision they are making that turns into habits. If I didn't break this pattern and continued to only work out when I felt like it, I would never be the leader I knew I was meant to be. I would never reach my potential.

What did I do to break the pattern? I began to repeat these mantras.

"Live by your principles. Not your feelings."

"Lead from your values. Not your circumstances."

Soon I was preaching at camps and posting on social media

the power of living these mantras.

Live by Your Principles. Not Your Feelings

Learning to live by your principles, not your feelings isn't easy to do. But there are things you can do to help you in this journey.

Saying No

We all have days when everything overwhelms us. We feel like the day is going 100 MPH and we have 97 things that need to be done NOW and 43 should have been done yesterday. You have to cultivate, through awareness, the ability to say "no" — to yourself and to others — and instead to take actions based on your core values, not on what you feel like doing. You have to learn to live with the fear of chaos. As Greg McKeown says in his book, *Essentialism*, "You are always going to make tradeoffs." Instead of asking, "How can I get all of this done," you need to be asking, "What do I want to trade?"

Taking Care of Yourself

Do you value your body, your health, and your well being? If you don't you'll never be able to make the impact you want. It starts with you. It starts with making daily investments in yourself. If not, you will get caught up in doing what you feel, not what your values dictate. To be the best version of yourself, you must do that which will help you evolve:

1. Practice great self-talk
2. Exercise
3. Meditate daily.

Values…Not Circumstances

To truly lead from our core values and principles, we have to be aware of them. They have to be concrete. They have to be a part of who we are and what we stand for and really believe in.

How can we achieve this?

By being mindful of how we feel, detaching from situations and looking at them objectively.

In this mindset, we are more likely to lead from our values because we are able to *react* to situations instead of *responding* to them

Mindfulness Increases Collaboration

When we see ourselves as separate from our ideas and actions — when we don't define ourselves by them — it's easier to look at situations non-judgmentally. How does this make a difference in leading an organization? It's easier to separate our egos and past decisions and put the needs of the people we lead first. It's a cliché but true — when no one cares who gets the credit, the best work gets done. When you care about doing what's best for the organization and your people, you allow your employees to put their ideas forth without fear of being shot down by negativity or your ego. You don't care where the ideas come from. And it all starts with the ability to be vulnerable.

Vulnerability

Vulnerability is not a weakness — it's a strength. Being vulnerable means that you don't become emotionally attached to an idea because it was *your* idea. It means you are okay getting insight and valuing the opinion of others while maintaining the courage and confidence to do what you, as the leader believe is right.

Leading with Integrity

When things go bad, do you react, or do you lead? Do you base your decisions on your values or on make more selfish decisions? In other words, do you honor your values?

In our business, we make every effort to stick with our values even if it means loss of revenue. We only want to work with kids who have a passion for basketball. Even when business hasn't been so great, we've turned kids (and lots of money) away, telling parents that we didn't think it was a good investment of their money and time because their son or daughter didn't seem that interested in getting better. Kids might tell their parents they are interested... they tell their parents what they want to hear... they want to make them happy. But their actions tell a completely different story. We want kids to find that thing that makes them put forth effort to being the best at "it." Our values are about inspiring people to pursue their potential doing something they love — even if it's not basketball.

Even When They Can't Do Anything For You

Leading from your values instead of your circumstances means treating people the same regardless of how your day has gone. It means treating people well even if they can't do anything for you.

And, this can come with a challenge. But when you become more mindful, you become aware of how you are actually behaving and are able to take the steps to change actions. Initially, you find it tough to treat people this way consistently and every day. But that's how great leaders impact the most lives – by how they treat people.

Chapter 17

THE INCREDIBLE POWER OF DETACHMENT

By now you know that yoga, meditation, and mindfulness have had a huge impact on my life. And, even though yoga has become increasingly popular for the masses due to the physical benefits, the biggest advantage is the bridge it creates between the physical and mental — the awareness it creates, and the power that this awareness gives you.

One of the best byproducts of this awareness it helps you emotionally detach from your thoughts and feelings. It creates a distance between stimulus and response — making it easier to handle really difficult, emotional decisions.

Because it's not necessarily the situation, emotion or material thing that matters, it's the emotional attachment and story that we associate with it.

And until we can completely detach from the situation, emotion, or material thing we can't be fully present with it. This is the only way to actually see clearly.

"You need to breathe <u>with</u> the emotion; you don't need to breathe it away." - Pema Chodron

So instead of just reacting to things, like a guy cutting you off when you're already late for work or school, you are able to intentionally respond. You're able to take a breath and rethink/ regroup. You're not going to let one guy start a snowball effect that is going to ruin rest of your day. What you're doing is detaching the emotion from the situation. The last time a guy cut you off driving to work, you ended up missing the light, spilled coffee on yourself because you had to slam on the breaks, were late for work, and yelled at a co-worker because you were upset. But it doesn't mean that it's going to happen again. Mindfulness is the practice of non-judgment to seeing things for what they are. A guy cut you off. Nothing more. Nothing less.

You missed a shot. Nothing more. Nothing less. It doesn't mean that you're a bad shooter or you'll never make shots. It means you simply missed a shot.

One of the best pieces of advice I ever got regarding decision-making was this subtle, but important distinction:

"It's okay to make your decisions based on your emotions and how you feel. It's not okay to make emotional decisions." - Gordon Sisson

Not only does mindfulness help with emotional decisions, it helps you be calmer and have more clarity when going into potentially emotional and difficult conversations. In fact, not only does Russell Simmons (Run DMC/Def Jam) meditate every day, he does before every big meeting he has; his team even tells him they can tell if he hasn't. This gives you the ability to be more aware of other people's feelings and adapt your communication style to make the other person more comfortable with you or the situation. Like as a coach, teacher, or leader dealing with someone who works extremely hard, but just isn't getting the job done. Those are difficult conversations. But, it's an investment — just like basketball skill development, getting stronger, or losing weight. You aren't going to see results right away, but you'll be able to have deeper, more significant, more impactful conversations down the road.

This emotional detachment also creates the awareness to help you see passing thoughts as states of mind. Just because you are angry, upset, or sad, doesn't mean you are an angry, upset, or sad person. By detaching these thoughts and seeing them for what they are — just thoughts — we don't label ourselves as this type of person. We don't start to tell ourselves the story that we are a loser, a quitter, or unworthy.

The stories we tell ourselves are so powerful because they literally help our brains develop how we feel about ourselves. We learn by them — it's how knowledge was originally passed on to others.

And these stories we tell ourselves affect how we feel, think, and act – and become the stories of our lives.

So stop. Sit. And breathe.

Remove the emotion and create a gap between what happens to you and your response.

"For example, anger comes up, and then you go to breathing as a way to chill out the anger. But you also want to really experience the underlying energy of anger until it no longer has this power over you." - Pema Chodron

Chapter 18
THE COMPOUND EFFECT

After reading hundreds of books on success, leadership, and personal development I finally came across the answer I have been searching for. It is one of the secrets to achieving big dreams and yet it is easy to do – and easy not to do. It also can work for you or against you without ever knowing it — until it hits you hard! The great thing though is that we ALL can harness its power. We can all choose to use it each and every day.

The problem is, we don't necessarily need <u>more</u> knowledge. With the information age, there is an abundance of knowledge out there on blogs, Twitter, YouTube, DVDs, books, and coaches clinics. If you're like me you have pages and pages of notes from attending practice sessions, workouts, and clinics. We all have the knowledge and some of us use it — for a short amount of time.

Several years ago I attended the Coach K and Duke Fuqua School of Business Leadership Conference in Durham, NC. There I met a successful, middle age man from South Carolina who started his own investment agency. We struck up a conversation on the second day when I said to him, " I don't mean to sound conceited, but a lot of the topics these presentations are on I've already heard or read before in books." He response was, "Most of us probably have, but few choose to take action with what we know. That's the hard part." What he said is absolutely true, but there was more to it than that.

While some people do take action with their knowledge few people take action with their knowledge <u>consistently</u>. Why do you think a majority of people on exercise programs or diets fail? They start out great, but when they don't see results immediately they quit. It's unending persistence that creates this consistency. Success is not a Lean Cuisine meal ready in 3.5 minutes.

A perfect basketball example is when we have a player come to us who needs to change his shooting form. We film their shot, break it down, and send them home with a program to use. A week later they come back and it looks GREAT! Sometimes I can't believe how much better their shot looks in only a week. Then another week goes by and they come back for an evaluation. Their shot looks like garbage. The first thing I ask them is if they followed the program that they did the first week and the first thing I hear is " Well..." or "I was but..." Why is this? I'm sure you guessed it but they didn't <u>consistently</u> follow the program that we gave them. At this point you are essentially back at square one.

Earlier, I said this secret could either work for you, or against you.

At the start of week 2 of the shooting program the player decides they are going to take Monday off. It won't matter, I'll make up for it Tuesday," they say. And you know what? Does it really matter that they took off Monday? Can you significantly tell that there is a difference in your shot from Sunday to Tuesday? Probably not. But Tuesday, you only do the required amount and don't make up what you missed. Wednesday, you really, really try to make up what you missed on Monday, but you only get 25% of Monday's workout done. Thursday rolls around and in Math class you "suddenly realize" there is a big test on Friday, so of course you can't go to the gym that night, even though you also realize your teacher announced the test two weeks ago. You miss Thursday as well and since you were up all night and exhausted from studying from the exam you decide that it's ok to take off Friday because "academics come first." It's a series of small choices that add up over time, which add up to achieving those big-picture goals.

I tell players: when practice is over, if you get a teammate, or setup the Dr. Dish, you'll get up approximately 200 shots. It will only take about 20 minutes and it's easy to do (and easy not to do!) Most teammates will leave and go home, which is easy to do. If they decide to stay and get up the extra 200 shots by the end of the week that will be 1,000 extra shots. At this point you probably will not be much better – you might not even see a difference. Don't quit, though, because at the end of the month that will be 4,000 extra shots if you do this just 5 days per week. You can even shoot before games on game day.

By now you probably are going to see a positive change, you feel much more in rhythm and your confidence should be up. But think – what if I just did this for the entire season – approximately 4 months. By the end of the season you would have shot an extra 16,000 shots and if you bring 3 other teammates that's 64,000 shots for your teammates come playoff time!

Will you get better if you do this workout? Absolutely! Will 95% of people choose not to do it? Most likely. This simple workout would take you 20 minutes each day. Simple to do, and simple not to do.

This secret is called the 'Compound Effect,' which I learned from Darren Hardy, publisher of SUCCESS Magazine. You are either getting better or getting worse — you don't maintain.

Call it persistence, call it consistency, call it the compound effect — whatever you want. But you won't make changes in your life until you change something that you do consistently. And mindfulness creates the awareness to see where you are developing habits and making these choices. It's the key to achieving big dreams and most people choose not to do it. But, in the end it's a choice — YOURS.

Chapter 19
WHY EVERYONE SHOULD BE A MODEL

Many people think that work ethic can't be taught. I completely disagree. I believe almost everything is learned somewhere, somehow, even if we don't consciously know it. As Swedish psychologist K. Anders Ericsson states in <u>The Talent Code</u>: "We're pre-wired to imitate. When you put yourself in the same situations as an outstanding person and attack a task they took on, it has a big affect on your skill." When have you ever seen a highly motivated employee or player under the supervision of a pessimistic, negative manager, parent or coach?

Modeling Behavior

A team is a reflection of their coach. If you want your players to remain calm and collected in pressure situations, you have to remain calm and collected. You can't scream at kids in a timeout and expect them to come out and execute a set you just drew up. It's a monkey see - monkey do world. Why? It's neuroscience. It's how we're wired. It's how we learn. Recent technological developments have allowed scientists to see what is exactly going on with the discovery of mirror neurons. These are specialized brain cells that can actually sense and then imitate the feelings, actions, and physical sensations of another person (Happiness Advantage).

If you want your kids to be professional, you have to act professional.

If you don't want your kids to drink alcohol, do drugs or smoke — you can't do it either.

If you want your players to tuck their jerseys in at practice — take a look at yourself. Does our staff have our shirts tucked in? Does our staff show up on time? Is our staff prepared for practice?

Are we working as hard on our "coaching game" as a staff as we are asking our players to work on their game?

If you don't want your kids get technicals and let themselves be affected by the calls in the game — look at yourself — are you?

The phrase, "Do as I tell you, not as I do," is the quickest way to lose trust and the ability to influence over your players.

As a staff, if we are asking our kids to be in the best possible shape that they can be in, are we making our health as a staff a priority? Players staying in shape make it easier for them to perform out on the floor, both mentally and physically. As a staff, if you are in better shape physically, it's going to allow you to handle more work (especially during the season), handle stress better, develop better practice plans, and make better decisions.

How do you handle losses? You're not very smart if kids don't know what you do after games to "handle" the loss. Are you down at the local watering hole drinking straight vodka or are you going out for a run, spending time with your family, or meditating? How would you want your players to respond?

Players absolutely love coaches that get out on the floor and sweat with them. You don't have to be a player. You just have to sweat, show effort and demonstrate your knowledge of the game. It shows that you are invested in them. You're not just a talking head telling them what to do.

Why do Shaka Smart's kids love him? He cares, he's invested, and they know it. I'm sure everyone remembers the video of him jumping in a drill during the Final Four a few years ago, making some closeouts, and then taking a charge to end practice.

What you do speaks so much louder than what you actually say. The people you lead may hear what you say, but they will feel your attitude.

When I was recruiting for the Wisconsin Playmakers (a club program I started), I was maybe 23 years old. A little kid compared to some of these high school coaches that I was trying to talk to in order to build a relationship and recruit their kids. I was recruiting a kid named Tommy Gaston from Adams-Friendship, WI. His high school coach was a guy by the name of Steve Klass who ran a 1-3-1 zone, demanded ball control, and went crazy when his kids made mistakes. I was scared shitless to go talk to this guy after the game to talk about a kid. But it turns out I met him outside after the locker room and he was extremely nice and helpful to me. Even after they lost.

We all say that our actions speak louder than words. So if we model this kind of body language around our kids, even if we are verbally positive with them, we're sending mixed messages. We are giving off a feeling to them that we are really disappointed in them, don't think they are good enough, or that they can't shoot. Being aware of your body language is paramount. Sometimes, we so caught up in the moment that we don't know how we are acting.

I've been very fortunate to be around positive people who modeled values and principles that have been infused in my character. For them, I will be forever grateful.

My Grandfather

When I was about 12 years old I remember spending time after school at my mother's parents' house and waiting for my grandfather to come home from work. He worked from 7 a.m.-3:30 p.m. at Felker Brother's Steel Factory in Marshfield, then spent he next few hours on his farm or a contractor project at someone's home. When he came home, the one thing I remember is him scrubbing his hands because they were absolutely filthy from working all day. He never complained, was happy to have his job, and was always happy to see me and my grandma. Usually these nights followed us watching the Bulls on WGN because my parents didn't have cable at the time. These were nights I never took for granted. But never knew the impact of seeing him grind it out every single day.

Forrest Larson

I had the best summer job in college you could ask for. I worked basketball camps for Forrest Larson, UW-Stout, Five-Star, and several other camps across the country. My summers were booked and I loved it. Working camps for Forrest taught me not only how to teach the game, but how to work. Truly work. He also taught me that you can live based on how you feel — you have to live by your principles. I specifically remember when we were about to start a camp up in Green Bay, WI, at the end of July. By this time of the summer he'd already been working camps for almost 8 weeks straight, 9 a.m.-9 p.m., with very few days off in between. He came up to me before we started the first session and said, "Mike, I am so 'camped out' right now". "Camped out" is a phrase we use when you are just exhausted from being on the floor all day long, demonstrating and playing defense. "Running this camp is the last thing I want to do right now." Three seconds later he blew his whistle, brought about 150 kids together, and gave his pre-camp speech and set expectations. His passion and energy was absolutely no different from the one he gave 8 weeks prior when we started our first camp session.

Andy Banasik

I've known Coach Banasik for over 20 years now, and even though he probably doesn't know it, he's had a huge influence on my life. Honestly, we haven't spent that much time together. I attended a couple camps of his in high school, he helped me with me shot a little and worked for him a couple weeks during his Prairie Du Chein Perimeter camps. But, the biggest impression he made on me was how I observed him: his work ethic, the way he treats people, and his passion. After working camp in college we'd workout, play pickup, or lift from about 9 p.m.-10:30 p.m. before heading in for the night. While Coach Banasik, who had been up before the sun, was making the rounds to all the gyms sweeping the floors and restocking refrigerators with Gatorade. His actions spoke louder than anything he could have ever said to me.

Dave MacArthur

Dave MacArthur, a varsity boys' coach at nearby Colby High School took me under his arm when I was a sophomore at

Marshfield Columbus. I don't have regrets, but if I could do one thing over it would have been to transfer schools to play for him. One of the greatest traits of leadership is to inspire, and that's exactly what he did. He possessed not only that, but enthusiasm, work ethic, and compassion, which gave him the ability to push people to their potential. I will never forget the days we spent in the gym when he pushed me so hard I felt like I was going to pass out. Those times taught me to do the same both on and off the court. Dave passed away tragically at the age of 36, but I only hope that I can continue to teach the way he taught me, and to influence, the way he influenced me.

Below is a short note I wrote that was displayed at his funeral services:

Influence

The ability to influence is regarded as one of the greatest traits of leadership. You possessed not only that, but enthusiasm, work ethic, and compassion, which gave you the ability to push people to their potential. I will never forget the days we spent in the Colby gyms. There were days I worked so hard that I didn't think I could take another shot, and then you pushed me some more. Those times taught me to do the same both on and off the court.

It was always enjoyable to watch your teams play because they were a direct extension of your work ethic and passion for the game. The same qualities you demonstrated on the sideline, your players demonstrated on the floor every time I came to watch. Each game I wanted to put on a Colby uniform and play just one minute for you. There is no doubt that your teams would have won state titles.

Even though your time in this world was limited, you made

an impact on us that takes many others a lifetime to achieve. I am grateful to have been one of those many lives that you touched. As I continue this life that you influenced me to lead, I only hope I can teach the way you taught me, and influence the way you influenced me.

You Get What You Model

When Dave was the Men's Basketball coach at UW-Marshfield, a junior college in Wisconsin, he coached the Marshfield High School boys' basketball team for the summer in leagues and tournaments. He would run some practices for them and always offered to work them out, "whenever you want. As long as I don't have something going on with my family I'll be there." So on a hot, muggy, midwestern summer night in July, at 1 a.m. one night, Dave's phone rang. It was one of the players from the Marshfield team. "Coach, can we get a workout in?" one of the kids asked, as Dave heard a couple of the others trying not to laugh in the background. "Yep, I'll be there in 15 minutes. You better be there." He hung up. Fifteen minutes later he was working out two of the players just like it was 1:15 p.m., not the middle of the night. Brad Fischer was there, now the UW-Oshkosh Women's Head Coach, remembers him getting after it, telling them, "No one else is working out right now." Music going and coaching them up, he was trying to motivate them to be the best possible version of themselves.

Brad says, "That one night has really influenced my coaching. You better backup and do everything that you say."

His assistant coach in high school, Rick Golz recalls, "Every time he saw you he greeted you like he cared, with energy and enthusiasm. He made you love life because he loved life."

You'll attract what you become.

The behavior you model is the behavior you will get. And the more you're aware of what you're modeling the more intentional you can be about your communication, actions and other behavior. You can model what you want your players to become. If you don't have this awareness to accurately perceive what you're modeling, you're going to be battling behaviors that aren't moving your team or organization towards your vision. Mindfulness creates this awareness.

Chapter 20
SPECIFIC AND SINCERE COMPLIMENTS

After running a preseason camp in Eau Claire, WI, my first hometown after college, I had a mom approach me. She introduced herself as Kelly and said her husband used to coach with Dave MacArthur. And then came the compliment I had never heard:

Kelly told me that Dave would tell her and her husband, "When I have kids I hope they have the passion and work ethic that Mike does. I'm really proud of him."

She had never met me before, but after watching me run camp and teach her kids she "knew exactly what Dave was talking about." It was the highest praise you could receive from someone. It wasn't about what you accomplished, the players you'd worked with or the games you'd won. It was about your character and who you were as a person.

Maybe it was just the timing, but I started to cry, and gave this woman I never had met before a hug. Dave had been a huge influence on me and it was the last camp I was running in Wisconsin, where I had built 3 organizations, before moving to Los Angeles. This move was a huge, but beneficial change that never would have been possible without Dave's mentoring. Since then, I've tried to be more mindful about the compliments I give. When you think about it, compliments like "great work" are so generic they aren't even heard through all the noise.

So I started to think, why don't we give more specific compliments? And, why don't I do it? I realized there was a certain uncomfortableness about it. In a weird way, it's kind of how you feel when you're sitting across from someone eating lunch, and they have blueberries from a smoothie stuck in their teeth. It's uncomfortable.

A specific compliment exposes you because it puts you in a place you have to be vulnerable. A sincere compliment is telling someone how you feel about what they've done. And everyone knows we all hate talking about feelings.

Mindfulness meditation makes us more vulnerable because we detach our feelings from who we are as a person. This gives us more confidence and makes us more comfortable to deal with situations that involve our emotions.

"When recognition is specific and deliberately delivered, it is even more motivating than money. Which is why encouragement and recognition should be used as rewards driving high performance, not just rewarding it." - Happiness Advantage

When I used to work summer basketball camps for Forrest Larson I remember him practicing this. During demonstrating an inside shoulder finish, he'd specifically tell me and everyone watching what I did well: "Great job initiating contact, putting your inside shoulder on the guy and taking him out of the play."

Another time I was running a ball-handling station and had somewhat deviated from the traditional. I added in a step to get players to start thinking about how their feet affected their ability to sell the crossover dribble.

"I really like what you did there, adding in that step. I think that is really going to help them understand the move. Great job."

How much harder do you think I worked after that? How do you think I felt? We all want to know what we are doing is contributing and making a difference. Specific feedback and recognition is a way to do this. And, being more vulnerable, telling people how you feel is a way to get there.

A common best practice in the business world is to "privately criticize — publicly praise," which is not so common in sports. But, legendary North Carolina Men's Basketball coach, Dean Smith, knew the power of authentically and specifically praising someone in front of their peers. He knew this could do wonders for their morale and also motivate other to follow this behavior. When he thought a player might be losing a little confidence he'd strategically design some sort of situation in practice to put this player in a position to do something well. It then gave him the ability to sincerely and specifically praise him in front of his peers. How about that mindful leadership?

A Harvard Business Review study shows that trying to change someone's skills, knowledge or work management is a lot easier than their attitudes, habits, or personality traits. So it's important to know what area you are giving someone feedback in. The way I see this is that we should use the first three — skills, knowledge, or work management — to build the relationship, connect, and invest in the player. Use this to build a foundation to be able to address their attitudes, habits or personality traits.

By practicing mindfulness you become more aware of the feedback your giving, and just as important, how you're giving it. Creating this awareness gives you the ability to construct it in a way that's going to motivate your people and produce results you want.

Chapter 21
THE MYTH OF MULTI-TASKING

We all want to get more done in less time. And, even though you'll never get it, I am pretty sure there is no one in the world who doesn't want more time.

In an effort to get more done we have become a culture of multi-taskers or should I say, task switchers. It's physiologically impossible to be fully concentrated on two different things at the same time. Your brain, actually is switching back and forth from one task to the other, without really being fully engaged in either of them. The problem lies in that it actually feels like we are doing more. Because we are. We are doing more, but we are being less productive. If you are taking notes on game film, then get a text on your phone which reminds you that you have to send an email to someone, then decide you have to refill your coffee, it actually takes more time to switch between all these tasks and get refocused on the game film you were watching. You might be doing more things, which makes you feel good, but in reality you're getting less done. All of the little interruptions add up.

For example, trying to watch ACC Sunday Night Hoops, while correcting papers that are due on Monday. I mean let's be real.

1) You aren't actually watching the game. You're trying to listen to it, and anytime the crowd gets loud or the color guy says, "Ohhh. What a move by..." you look up. Only it's too late to catch the play and you have to watch it on replay. I mean, why not just catch it on SportsCenter?

2) Every time you look up, or even if you hear something on the game, you lose track of where you were at in the paper. Studies show that anytime you are interrupted during a task, which requires serious focus and brain function, it takes a minimum of 10 minutes to be fully re-engaged in the process.

This is why a couple years ago I shut off the email notifications on my phone. And more recently completely shut off my phone and any notifications on my computer when working on a project.

Here are few examples of task switching that literally can be fatal.

Texting and driving. No explanation needed here.

Texting or Social Media during workouts. It's unreal how much I see players on social media or texting during camps or workouts. Every break or between sets they are on their phone.

Texting when trying to write a paper. If you are in the middle of formatting a concept and get a text it completely disengages you from the thought.

Responding to email while talking on the phone. This is one of my biggest and worst habits. Though I have gotten better at it, I never really was aware of how bad it was until I started meditating. I have a horrible memory, but I think this was due way more to my habits of trying to multi-task in everything I did.

Can you clean and catch up on the phone, yes, of course.

Some activities, that are already habits, like walking your dog you can do two things at once. Studies show you are going to get much less enjoyment out of them, because you're not completely present in either.

By becoming fully engaged in a task, you are more likely to enjoy them, and do a better job completing them.

To become fully engaged in a task you have to risk the fear of chaos. Or perceived chaos. If you miss a text, an Instagram post, or a phone call it's not really that big of a deal. The challenge is that we are so bombarded with messages throughout the day we react to everything. And this reaction becomes a habit. Blocking out things like social media to work on your big picture dreams is what Greg McKeown, author of Essentialism, calls making tradeoffs. And the more tradeoffs we make the closer we'll be to achieving those dreams.

So if you are going to work, then work. If you are going to play, then play. The brain's natural state is one of peace and calm. It's not meant to function at 100 miles and hour in 1,000 directions. When you start to focus on one thing at a time and be great at it, that's when you start to have things build off of each other. You've started to initiate the Compound Effect.

Mindfulness gives us the ability to intentionally spend our time.

Are we spending our time in our areas of highest contribution?

Chapter 22

HOW GRATEFULNESS LEADS TO GREATNESS

This will come as a shock to some of my former players.

Even though they were in 7th grade, I treated them like they were playing college basketball. Practices were demanding and expectations were really high. So much that they even gave me the nickname Adolph. There was too much pressure and not enough love. I did what I thought was right at the time, but new experiences change your perspective and philosophy. When I started hot yoga to de-stress, workout, and rehab a hamstring injury, it led to a growing interest in meditation and mindfulness. And in yoga, there is a heavy emphasis on gratitude and being present, which I never tied together until recently. Being grateful can put you in a present state of mind.

Basketball is something you started playing because you enjoyed it — not because you wanted a college scholarship or to win player of the year in your league. You fell in love because of the pure joy that it brought you to play the game. And, contrary to popular belief, research shows that happiness actually breeds success — not the other way around.

When I brought mental performance coach Joshua Medcalf to our Coaches Academy in Milwaukee he said something about gratefulness that I had never heard before. And it hit home. Big time.

"We can tap into our greatness by being grateful."

When we change our mindset to gratitude we instantly go from a place of pressure, expectations, and outcome-based thinking, to an opportunity mindset. What else does it do? It allows us to step into that ever-elusive state of flow, or more commonly known as, "in the zone."

Why does gratefulness have this effect on this? According to Shayna Hiller, a Holistic Wellness Coach based out of Los Angeles, "Gratefulness puts us in the present because we focus on the things that are right in front of us. When we do this we can't have regret about the past or have anxiety about the future. We have to focus on the now because being grateful is about appreciating what you have right in front of you."

It also turns out that our brains are pre-wired to perform most efficiently when we are happy, and positive. Not neutral or negative. When our brains are scanning our environment to seek out the positive things, we automatically see more things that are positive.

Try this short visualization exercise first and take note of how you feel. Take three deep breaths, close your eyes, and visualize a game during the season as you normally would. The fans... the other team... the jump ball. And then feel stress, the pressure, the expectations.

Now visualize the same situation, but think about how grateful you are to be able to play... to be healthy, to compete, and to enjoy playing the game. You should literally feel yourself change to a more relaxed state. Yes it'll take time and something that you'll have to practice like anything else. But, after you consistently apply it you'll begin to see different results.

I challenge you to start each practice and game you participate in writing out one thing you are grateful for about the game.

Player: I'm grateful that my coach demands excellence of me.

Parents: I'm grateful my child has the opportunity to be a part of something much bigger than themselves.

Coaches: I'm grateful I'm in a position to positively impact lives.

The more you are aware of the good things in your life the more grateful you will become. And, this increase in gratitude will allow you to see more good things. There are tons of studies out there about how gratitude increases happiness. But, where does it start? By being aware of what is in front of you in this current moment.

Tap into your gratitude, get present and step into your greatness.

Chapter 23
EXPECTATION HANGOVERS

"We suffer when our reality does match the expectations we are so attached to." - Christine Hassler.

As players and coaches, we suffer from so many unmet expectations that are completely outside our control. There are obvious ones like making shots and winning, but take rebounding for example. Many coaches have a couple expectations regarding this:

"Control the boards."

"We can run if we don't rebound."

"We need 12 offensive rebounds every game."

These are expectations some coaches set, but in reality they are out of the players' control. What they <u>can</u> control is watching the flight of the ball, trying to predict where it might hit the rim, and attacking the ball. They can control making contact and boxing out. But they can't control rebounding.

It's not that expectations are bad. It's that our expectations should be controllable — not outcome-based — ones like awards, stats, or scholarships. We can control our effort, our mindset and how good of a teammate we are.

And, as a parent these are the things you should be asking

your kids: Did you work hard? Were you a good teammate?

When I read Christine Hassler's book, <u>Expectation Hangover</u>, I only wish she would have written years ago. I highly suggest it for any coaches who have expectations to win, players feeling pressure to perform or parents who have any kind of outcome-based expectations for their kids.

"Not clinging to fixed ideals helps you see more clearly because your vision is not obstructed by fear or desire." - Christine Hassler

Through mindfulness we begin to develop a better sense of what type of expectations are within our control.

Some things are more obvious, like the examples above, but when it comes to leadership or coaching roles there is a lot of grey area. Every single person you are leading or are in a relationship with has a unique set of experiences that has led them to this point in their life. Practicing mindfulness gives you the ability to have the compassion, understanding and empathy to set healthy boundaries and expectations within the other person's control.

Chapter 24
THE POWER OF NOW

Happiness can't exist at the same time as regret or worry.

And as we learned earlier happiness is a predictor of success — not the other way around. You can't be afraid of the past and at the same time still be in the present moment.

Unless you are completely in a meditative state your mind is focusing on one of these three things below at all times. And, in order to tap into the power of mindfulness, it's important to understand them

Past: Regret, shame or guilt

Present: Focused on task at hand

Future: Worry is a preoccupation of the mind about an anticipated negative event or catastrophic outcome

Past

Regret is a hard place to live. Regret, more than guilt, can drift into becoming an internal state, which sadly dominates life. Psychologist Carl Jung believes that, "Until you make the unconscious conscious, it will direct your life and you will call it fate."

After a successful senior year at Belmont University, Drew

Windler, player development coach, and performance training specialist at Thrive3, had several opportunities to play professional basketball overseas. But, it would have come at a cost. Yes, from the cultural point of view he would have been viewed as a success. But, he was able to separate himself from society's definition and look at what really made him happy to make his decision. He valued his relationships, family, and other activities he'd have to give up to go play overseas. When someone asks him why he didn't go play professionally he still has a little feeling of regret. But, because of the self-awareness he's created, Drew knows what truly matters in his life — putting him back in the present moment.

Future

Many of the performance related struggles come from being in the "Future" state of mind. While it's good to dream and have a vision we can be affected in three different ways when worrying about the future.

1) Physiologically we experience things like clammy hands, dry throat, sweating, and increased heartbeat when we are faced with things like a big game, test, meeting, or important client phone call.

2) Cognitively we have thoughts about what <u>could</u> go wrong. I might turn the ball over, miss this shot, or get pulled out of the game. I might not win this conference championship. If I don't, I'm a failure.

3) Avoidance surfaces when we are trying to learn a new skill. So many times people give up, or don't even try at something because they are afraid to fail. They aren't in an environment that views failure and mistakes as learning. Why do kids do this? Here's my one and only "Friday Night Lights" reference:

"I used to never want anything because wanting meant trying. I knew that if I tried I'd probably fail." - Tyra Collette

I'd say this holds true for the reason most people don't go after what they really want. They are afraid of external validation and what that says about them as a person.

Hope can also show up in this situation. But hope usually only prolongs misery or anxiety. It's action, even small steps, that lead us out. Why? Because it puts us in the present.

Worry also shows up as negative thinking in three different forms: overgeneralization, catastrophic thinking, or labeling.

Overgeneralization: Even though this has gotten better while practicing mindfulness, I do this a lot. It's going to extremes in your thinking. Remember in school when you had to correct each other's papers or essays? When you write something that you think is really good, and when your editing partner returns it to you, with only four edits in a 2-page paper, you think to yourself, "Well, my entire paper is awful." But you really only need to change a couple edits. Or even worse, you attach it to yourself and say, "My writing is awful," which is what most of us do. I see this all the time with kids who have a low level of confidence when it comes to shooting the basketball. They might be going through a shooting drill, and they miss 4-5 shots in a row, they're self-talk starts to be "I can't shoot." That's an extreme thought and generalization. You're basing your entire ability based on 5 missed shots and that significantly affects your confidence level.

Catastrophic thinking is also shows up when worrying. "I can't make a left handed layup, so I won't make the team. If I can't make the team, I won't have any friends, won't be popular, and won't get the girl that I want." This is thinking in extremes about possible outcomes in the future instead of seeing situations for exactly what they are. Maybe you aren't good with your weak hand, but that's the only fact. The others are assumptions about what might happen in the future.

Labeling is attaching meaning or judgment to some thing or situation. *I need these clothes in order to be popular. I need this job in order to be successful.* Or, they are "if then" statements. *If I don't make the team, then I am a failure. If I don't get this job, land this new client, or win this game I'm not a good person.* Mindfulness meditation allows us to detach from these situations and see them for what they are.

You might have been an assistant coach for 10 years and are getting your first chance to be a head coach at the varsity level. Only, it doesn't go as expected. You go 6-15 in your first year, your booster club fund is almost depleted and the player who is expected to be your go-to-guy moves because his dad got a new job. This doesn't mean you'll never win games, build a sustainable program, or have a great player in your program. You can label yourself a failure, or you can start to find the opportunities in the situations. You can learn new fundraising strategies, how to build a sustainable player development program, and different ways to evaluate your success than winning and losing.

No matter what it is, all of these are signs of fear or worry.

And the best thing you can do for your future self is to be present in this current moment.

Chapter 25
NICKELS AND DIMES

True Confidence

When we are directing Thrive3 workouts or events, we make a conscious effort, NOT to tell players what to do. We're not giving handouts. We're not giving nickels and dimes.

Great coaches, leaders, and teachers don't tell people what to do. They get them to think for themselves, come up with answers on their own, and empower them.

When we don't allow people to come up with their own answers, to determine what is right or wrong for them, they become resentful. They feel oppressed. That's the opposite of what true leadership is. We want them to feel empowered. This guidance also creates a level of respect. When people go through the struggle and find the answers on their own they are grateful that you didn't just provide them the solution. They start to value the struggle, view it as an opportunity to grow and realize it's the only way to really build confidence.

There are a lot of things that go into developing true confidence. You must work hard enough to truly deserve success and <u>believe</u> that you deserve success. You need to be aware of the thousands of thoughts that go through your mind each day. And, then, change your self-talk to be positive, or better yet, just seeing them as thoughts. In the end, yes, it's on the individual person to internalize these beliefs, but if you're a coach or mentor, you might be the catalyst.

How are handout culture is killing confidence

I'm a firm believer that handouts don't work. Actually, I don't just believe this. It's the truth. They do not work.

Your efforts have to move beyond trying to make yourself and the people you are trying to help feel better. It has to be an effort of empowerment and creating ownership.

The problem lies in that, while it makes the giver feel good in the short-term, it's only a band-aid to cover up the problem. And, it has long-term negative consequences by creating a co-dependent behavior, always expecting something because they start to define themselves by their circumstances. Underlying this entitlement mindset is a mind full of guilt, shame, and scarcity. In this environment people get good at getting things for free. It's crazy how many parents have told me, "Well, we just don't pay for anything," or "we can't afford it." But, you can afford that Range Rover and a new pair of Jordan's every 6 weeks? Our basketball culture and government system has created a huge problem — instead of assisting and empowering, we are enabling. And it has created generations looking for something for free.

We also seem to have a huge problem with confidence and self-esteem in this country — especially in the inner-city and other low socio-economic environments. When we just give someone the answers, service, or product we don't allow them to struggle through the ups and downs. They don't value it because they don't pay for it — financially, or with their time and hard work. And, obviously there are multiple issues here, but the problem is we give too many handouts. People become dependent on them without having to go through the struggle of truly working through something. Without going through the struggle you can't develop the confidence to believe that you deserve what you are working for. If you don't believe in yourself, this becomes a cycle of dependence. You're looking for something outside of your control to make you feel better about yourself.

Case in point: participation awards. One of my friends from college posted a picture on Facebook of his daughter after her first gymnastics class. What was she holding? A participation ribbon. Why did we start giving these awards? No, it wasn't to make the participant feel better. It was to make it easier for the teacher or leader who is handing these out. It's a lot easier to handout a ribbon than it is to try and get your people to understand that it's okay to fail, to make mistakes, and that the process is what truly matters. In life we don't get rewarded for participation, but that's exactly what we are teaching our kids. You get rewarded for putting forth your best effort, over and over again, until you become proficient at something. Maybe we should be giving out "True Effort" awards instead of participation?

At our DRIVE Summer Academy we have what we call a "Swag Bag" with Elite Socks, shorts, and other Nike gear from Footlocker House of Hoops. A lot of summer camps will give out items, almost like a lottery system, but what we've done different is instead of just giving things away, we reward behaviors. Things players can control. We pick out specific things that players do, like doing a great job encouraging other players or getting out of their comfort zone. These expectations are communicated before we start the Academy so we tie our expectations to what gets rewarded. If you want to repeat or increase these behaviors your people should always know exactly what they are being rewarded for. That's a big difference from handouts.

Assist Without Enabling

"I got a problem with the handouts, I took the man route. I'll give an opportunity though, that's the plan now." - Jay-Z, Nickels and Dimes

From a leadership perspective it's a lot easier to just give someone you care about the answer than to see them struggle through the ups and downs on their own. The more we care about them, the more compassionate and empathetic we are, the harder it is to see them struggle. It becomes really hard for us to separate sympathy and empathy.

But, real leaders can separate their emotions from the struggle and challenge the person to do more and become more. So mindfulness does two things here.

It allows us to detach emotionally from the struggle of the person we are leading. We need to be empathetic enough to understand, but strong enough not to be attached.

It also gives us the patience to not just throw them the answer. It gives us the patience and consciousness to ask the right questions, get them to think for themselves and to come up with the answers on their own. It teaches them that it's okay to fail and that it is <u>their</u> journey. They don't have to live it for someone else.

Enable someone and you create a codependent cycle of disappointment, guilt, and shame.

Empower them and you're a catalyst for responsibility, growth and change.

As a leader, teacher, parent, or coach it's on you to see the difference and be mindful about how your actions are influencing the people you lead.

Chapter 26
IGNITION

I'm not someone who believes inspiration comes from within. Motivation does, but not inspiration. Somewhere along the way someone has inspired you. They've seen potential in you that you weren't able to see yourself. But the true influencers don't tell you how great you already are. They tell you how great you could be. They see beyond where you're currently at. They can see past the mistakes, through their flaws and can see their potential. And, then they paint a vivid, detailed vision of what you could become through hard work, persistence and patience.

In the end, when the game is on the line, you must have an unwavering confidence to make the right play or right decision as a parent or leader. But, where does this all begin? Does this belief and sense of confidence come directly from inside the mind of the person? Or does someone need to paint a picture of your future before you will actually start to internalize what you could become?

While the "final say" has to do with you, I think 99% of the time it's ignited by someone or something else. The stories to follow will explain why. And, after reading, I think you'll agree.

In Daniel Coyle's excellent book, <u>The Talent Code</u>, he calls this 'Ignition.' If you are in 7th grade and see a player from your high school team go on to play college basketball, you might start to think, "if he can do it, why can't I?" We come from the same place, go to the same school, and will have the same coaches. If he can do it, I can, too. This is exactly the feeling I got when I was in 7th and 8th grade watching my high school basketball team win back-to-back State Championships. And, I saw the best player, Jason Linzmeier, go on to play in college. As a leader it's your responsibility to assist in ways like this. Find ways to assist through inspiration not through power or authority, which ultimately drain your energy and are not long lasting.

Jay Bilas tells a story in his book, <u>Toughness</u>, a must-read for coaches and parents. After his sophomore year in high school he was scheduled to have his wisdom teeth removed the 2nd day of the USA Olympic development team tryouts in Los Angeles, attracting some of the best players in the area. His dad encouraged him to at least attend the first day of tryouts, knowing he wouldn't be able to make it the second day.

According to Bilas, he showed up, played hard and, "certainly hadn't embarrassed myself, which was my only real goal." Leaving the gym, a legendary writer in the southern California high school basketball community, said to Bilas, "See you tomorrow." As Bilas explained to him that he wouldn't be able to make it because of his appointment, the writer turned to his dad and said, "You might want to reschedule that appointment. Your son was the best player in the gym today." Bilas claims this was the most powerful moment in his basketball career and helped develop his belief in himself. Yes, ultimately he put the work in to be able to get to that level, it came from him, but it was ignited and uncovered by someone else.

Would this statement have been powerful and long lasting if Bilas hadn't been a relentless worker and deserved success? Most likely not. But it's the right words, by the right person, in the right situation that can ignite this journey.

Another example of ignition from the 2012-13 NBA season is the shooting performances of the Golden State Warriors' Klay Thompson and Steph Curry. Jon Berry, NBA analyst, commented in a playoff game that "Mark Jackson's (Warriors coach) confidence in their ability has such an impact on their game." Berry stated, "He (Jackson) says they are 2 of the best shooters in the history of the game. Even if he doesn't really believe it he gets them to believe it." Again, without hours and hours in the gym would this be the case? Probably not.

Chapter 26
HOW TO VIEW PRESSURE AS AN OPPORTUNITY

Mindfulness gives us more clarity when dealing with pressure situations because it gives us the ability to detach emotionally and be better at perceiving reality. Reality is only what we perceive. And we always have a choice. Here's what I mean:

Imagine you walk into a bank where there are 50 other people. Suddenly a bank robber walks in, fires his weapon once to get everyone's attention, and you are hit by the shot in your arm. He robs the bank teller and proceeds out of the bank. If you were describing this event to your friends at school or co-workers the next day, would you describe it as lucky or unlucky?

This is a situation that author, Shawn Anchor, poses to executives in his training sessions. Usually the response is 70% = unlucky and 30% = lucky. I'll admit, when I first read this in his book, The Happiness Advantage, I was shocked. How in the world do 30% of people feel that this is lucky?! While it is unfortunate to be shot anywhere, it turns out that there are many other alternatives. You could have been shot in the head, paralyzed, or he could have fired multiple shots injuring someone next to you that you love. It's our choice to see what we want.

Here are some specific situations:

What You Perceive

Being able to perceive reality also puts us in a position where we are able to choose how we view pressure situations. In almost every single basketball pressure situation there is a negative and positive consequence. But we always have a choice how we view this situation. It's the reason why certain people want to take game winning shots and others would rather be on the bench. It's how we perceive the situation.

There is the story we are telling ourselves, based on our past experiences and failures. And then there is what is the truth. What is *actually* happening.

And, by being aware of how we actually perceive something we can train our mind to look for what we want.

Back in the age of the saber tooth tiger, we developed a sense of fear in order to survive in a dangerous world. That fight or flight response warned us of clear and present danger just like an animal might. Now, 99% of the time, this physiological process is irrelevant. Our biology hasn't caught up with society's advancements. We don't have to worry about bears attacking us in the middle of the woods. We worry about the consequences of missed shots, lost games, and whether or not that cute boy or girl across the room is into us. These are obviously not life-or-death issues.

Instead we are afraid of these outcomes, only because of the meaning we attach to them. Because you miss a shot doesn't mean you can't shoot. Because you lose a game doesn't mean you are a loser. Because you can't get the attention of that cute boy or girl on the basketball team doesn't mean there isn't someone else. It's not the outcome — it's the meaning we attach to it.

And we fear this because we let these meanings and outcomes define who we are at our core. Who we are as a human being. And that is the scariest question of all. Who am I? What do I mean in this world?

"I think it's easy for people to confuse inner peace and you being comfortable with who you are with complacency. And it's the exact opposite. Because when you're focused on the moment, and each day as it comes, when the big moment comes and everybody's looking at you, you're really ready, because you really just looked at it as one day at a time." - Kobe Bryant

The problem is, our genetics have not caught up with modern times. We are drawn to things that bring out fear in us because before it was necessarily for our survival. But now, all it does is fill us with fear, worry and anxiety. Through mindfulness we learn to see that we are separate from our actions, fears and feelings. We are so much more than that.

Chapter 28

YOUR 5 GREATEST INFLUENCES

Awareness gives you the ability to see what actually is influencing you. And one of the best ways to tap into this awareness is to perform an input audit.

Consider this: What are the things that we read, watch, listen to, people we surround ourselves with, and the environment that we are in? Once we consider each, we need to rate on a scale of 1 - 10, how these inputs are contributing to the greater purpose in my life? You'll see that with every single one of these inputs you have a choice. Unless you are in school and have to follow a curriculum you have a choice in every type of content that you consume. What you consume affects your thoughts. Your thoughts affect how you feel. Your feelings determine your choices and these choices become habits. These habits determine who you become and what you accomplish.

- Who do you surround yourself with: teammates, co-workers, friends?
- What do you watch: tv, online, movies)?
- What do you read: books, online content?
- What do you listen to: podcasts, audiobooks, music?

- Your environment: neighborhood, school, workplace?

Who Do Your Surround Yourself With?

You have to ask yourself, are these things I'm consuming and surrounding myself with having a beneficial impact on my life? If they aren't you need to cut them out. Even if it's your friends.

Yes you really do need to unfriend and unfollow people in real life.

I was watching former Arkansas governor, Mike Huckabee's show several years ago, and he had a guest on talking about association by assimilation. While this is not an innovative concept he said it in a way I have never heard before; I think makes it a lot easier for kids to pick up. The guest was Elvis Presley's step-brother, who talked about Elvis' downfall and ultimately his death. He said that Elvis was truly a good guy, but surrounded himself with the wrong people. Since then his message to kids has been, "show me your friends I'll show you your future." So true.

Jim Rohn, one of America's foremost business philosophers, lived by this philosophy when it came to people. He called it the 'Rule of 5.' You will become the average of the 5 people you surround yourself with the most. That is some truthful and powerful stuff.

Whether you believe it or not, the people you surround yourself with have a significant impact on your choices, hopes, dreams, and desires.

Is it possible to achieve your goals and still hangout with people who drink, stay out late, and don't have the same dreams as you? Yeah, you can, but it's hard as hell. How much easier is it going to be to get up in the morning to train before school if you do it with at least 1 other person chasing the same dreams?

Don't have something to do? Start something like a Friday night workout club, be a leader, and take ownership.

How much easier would it be to achieve your dreams if you surrounded yourself with people who wanted to achieve the same things that you did? I pretty much had zero people in my high school besides a couple kids in my younger brother's class who wanted what I did. It was extremely frustrating. But once I found other kids from other schools in my area it became so much easier. It's easier socially and easier for working out. Instead of going to a party on Friday night, we would stay at the gym and play 1-on-1.

If your goal is to play college basketball or beyond, or even just make your high school team, doesn't it make sense to surround yourself with people who want the same things? Ones who want to go to the gym, workout, and make the right choices about drugs and alcohol?

Or are your friends the ones that are out drinking on the weekends, chasing girls or only work on their game the week before the season starts?

Wouldn't it be easier to live your dreams when you have people around you constantly reminding you to do the right thing?

Show me your friends I'll show you your future.

What about the information you read?

What we read can be anything from Twitter, Facebook, a book, to the newspaper.

Are you reading People, Cosmo, Maxim and BuzzFeed? "If you feed your mind with trash you'll get trash results." - Jim Rohn

Who do you follow on Twitter, Instagram, and Facebook? Are they things that are having a beneficial impact on your life? How about following people like Jon Gordon, Joshua Medcalf, Alan Stein, Drew Hanlen, or Kevin Eastman? People who are going to feed your mind with knowledge and provide tools for you to achieve your dreams.

What do you listen to?

Music, Podcasts, Audiobooks, Radio Talk Shows

I have an unwritten rule. Anytime in the car if I'm driving more than 20 minutes to a location I'm listening to a podcast. Motivational speaker, Zig Ziglar, called this "Automobile University."

I used to be in my car all the time. Throughout the year I put about 20,000 miles on my car traveling for basketball events and I used to spend most of that on the phone or listening to music.

Several years ago I was working out a high school team, 30 minutes from home at 6 a.m. so there wasn't anyone available to talk to. So one day I decided to download a couple of Kevin Eastman's free podcasts available on his website. It was short, but it was so much better than listening to morning talk shows or music. This led me to download an audio book featuring 15 hours of Zig Ziglar and Jim Rohn. Ziglar mentioned how much time you spend wasting in your car. He said everyday he gets in his car and attends automobile university on his way to work or meetings.

"A study by the University of Southern California revealed that if you live in a metropolitan area and drive 12,000 miles a year you can acquire the equivalent of two years of college education in three years' time by listening to educational information in your car. Since the average American adult spends from two hundred to seven hundred hours each year in an automobile, this is good news." - ZigZiglar.com

If you have an average drive of 30 minutes a day, that's 150 minutes a week or 2.5 hours that you spend in the car. That's 125 hours per year that you can be filling up your mental factory.

What do you watch?

I used to watch the news every night before I went to bed. It is almost a tradition in America. I got hooked on "Anderson Cooper 360" — timely, compelling stories told to update you about what is going on in the world. It made me feel good to be "educated" and current on things.

Is it important to stay informed? Yes. We should know what's going on in the world, but not to the point where it consumes us. For me, social media is enough. If something happens I should know about, most likely someone I'm following is either talking about it or retweeted it. If they aren't — it probably doesn't affect me.

Am I against watching TV, movies, or consuming content on the internet? No, of course not. But you have to be mindful about what you are consuming. Now, I'll be the first to admit: Netflix is a blessing and a curse. It definitely has cut a little into my reading time at night, but "New Girl" might be the funniest show I've ever see and how can you not watch "MadMen?"

I was going to write this myself, but Darren Hardy says it best:

"Early on, I learned the difference between THE world and MY world. I only pay attention to MY world. After all it's the only thing I can do anything about. Paying too much attention to the rest of it only makes me feel fearful, frustrated and cynical.

"All I have in life is my attention. I have to make a choice of where I give it. That choice affects my experience of life and determines my potential for positive creativity. I can focus it on the worst of the world or the best. I can focus it on things I can't do anything about or I can focus it on those things that I can and that have a direct on my life and my family.

"So, until the war comes marching up my street, I'm not paying much attention to it. Until Al Qaeda knocks on my door and threatens my family, I'm not tracking their development. Until the earthquake is under my foundation or the tsunami rolls up my driveway, I'm not giving it my time. Murders, rapes, scandals, break-ins... I'm not interested."

Environment

This can be hard to define sometimes because it gets tied into who we surround ourselves with. I'm going to define it as a physical space. I used to really care less about about how clean my home was, unless I had friends coming over. But, when I started to become more mindful of how things felt I realized I felt much calmer, focused, and relaxed when my place was clean. When I'm in an organized, clean environment, which might be your desk space in your office, I find it much easier to be productive. I realized later on that's why I loved boutique hotels, yoga studies and other physical spaces with great design. It was about how it made me feel.

Wrap Up

How are you supposed to face each day with a positive, opportunistic attitude if you are reading the news about the wars, economy, and crime?

What if you surround yourself with negative people who suck

your energy and are always complaining about trivial things like the traffic, which you have absolutely zero control over?

Again, our brains are prewired to search out fear — it was built into our DNA for survival, but we no longer need to be afraid of the saber tooth tiger. The way you think is affected by what you put into your mind. What you read, watch, and listen to drastically affects your thinking.

"Our lives are most affected by the way we think they are – not the way they are." - Jim Rohn.

Why is this important? What we consume significantly influences how we think.

And we literally do become what we think.

Chapter 29

CREATING AN INTENTIONAL LIFE

Time. It is literally all we have. George Raveling, Director of International Basketball for Nike says, "I don't understand when people say they don't have time. All you have is time." It's not about time. It's about how we use it. And, being mindful gives you the ability to see where you are exactly spending your time.

Does the time you spend align with your dreams? Or are you spending time on things that don't really matter?

What is the best use of my time right now to make the maximum impact? I ask myself this all the time and it's what I use to prioritize things.

If we spend our time doing things based on how we feel, we will always be doing the things that are urgent. The things that, in the long run, won't make that big of a difference. The ones that won't close the gap between where we are, and where we want to be. And, more important, who we are and who we want to be.

You have to be able to live with the fear of chaos.

"When you strive for greatness, chaos is guaranteed to show up. In fact, other areas of your life may experience chaos in direct proportion to the time you put in on your ONE Thing." - Gary Keller

I have two lists that I work from every week. One is my ONE Thing list, which I adopted from The ONE Thing by Gary Keller. The other side of the paper is my "Investments in Impact List." I don't call it my task list. Your task list gives the impression they are just things you have to get done; they don't have a purpose. I only put things on this list that are going to move me forward towards making an impact. They might not be things that directly relate to making an impact, like doing my taxes, but that's something that I just have to get done in order to continue to run our business. There isn't any way around it. So by doing my taxes I'm shifting my mindset. It's changing my perception. I can view it as a task that sucks and has to get done or I can view it as something that allows me to do what I love and make an impact. The choice is always yours.

In Essentialism, by Greg McKeown, he calls this 'making tradeoffs.' Every single thing we decide to do is a tradeoff and makes an impact in a different area of your life. Socially, physically, mentally...everything is a tradeoff and it's up to you where you want to make the most impact in any given moment.

Being aware of our time also gives us the ability to see where we are exactly spending it. It will give you a much clearer picture of how you are spending your 84,600 seconds each day. It's shocking when you actually break down what we do with our time. Most likely you will find that you have some major time sucks because if you're like most people, you don't use your time very intentionally. One of my time sucks is Social Media. While it's part of our business and we need to engage with followers, I don't think my time spent on it is in proportion to the results we get from it. I spend way too much time scrolling through pointless updates, images, and videos.

It's a pretty big eye opener for players when we talk about this at events. Most of them how no clue that they usually have 7+ hours each day where they can decide what they do with their time. We break it down for them from the time they get out of school until the time they go to sleep. If you are serious about chasing your dreams here is what a sample after-school schedule should look like.

3 pm-3:30pm: Refuel, Rehydrate, Meditate
3:30 pm-5pm: Skills Work
5 pm-6 pm: Strength and conditioning work
6 pm-7 pm: Dinner
7 pm-9 pm: Homework*
9 pm-11 pm: Relax, movies, social media, video games

Most have no clue that they can spend 2.5 hours working on their game and still have 5 hours for homework, dinner, and social time.

Here is where you lose time during those 8 hours after school

1) Social Media, Phone, Texting during workouts
2) Working on your dunks after workouts
3) Socializing during your lifts
4) Not getting to your post school routine of Refuel, Rehydrate, and Meditate right away. If you get sucked into what everyone else is doing after school you'll be stuck in limbo. You'll be trading what you want at the moment (socializing, being a normal kid) for what you want the most (reach your potential at something

you love)

This is why it's crucial to surround yourself with people who are chasing the same dreams as you.

*Now, keep in mind that this is just an average. I did put homework at the end of the night because I think after sitting classrooms all day long you need a break. After a workout and dinner you have your blood flowing, new oxygen to your brain and should be relaxed and alert to focus on what you need to.

Want to add another hour of your day to this? Do your strength workout before school. You'll be a lot more awake and alert during school and might even enjoy your classes more. Just don't crush donuts after your workout.

Chapter 30
HOLD THE VISION. TRUST THE PROCESS.

Mindfulness also gives us the ability to focus on the process because it helps us be more present. This is huge, because many times, when we don't achieve the results we want, it's not that we aren't putting forth effort, it's that our efforts are not focused and intentional.

We all know that focusing on winning doesn't help us win games. It's about focusing on the things in a game within our control that put us in the best possible position to execute our game plan and play to our potential. So instead of focusing on making shots, taking care of the ball and playing defense are where our focus should be. We need to be as detailed as possible with the teaching points we are trying to execute.

- Making shots we are focused on, being on balance, shoulders over knees over toes and following through straight to the rim.
- Are we focusing on taking care of the ball or are we focusing on throwing hand-to-hand passes, passes to the receiver outside shoulder (under pressure), making a rip pivot and maybe a

second pivot.

- Are we telling our kids that we need to defend or are we telling them we need to close out short on players who can't shoot, don't help off shooters in the corner and always rotate into the basketball?

- Are we telling our players to "stop thinking and play the game?" This might be the worst advice I've ever given a player. Even though I hated it when a coach said it to me, I said it to players I coached because I just couldn't figure out a different solution. It was purely out of habit. I'm wondering if that truly has ever worked for anyone? I know it absolutely never worked for me.

Until now, I never had a tool or exercise to actually get players to "stop thinking and play the game." Practicing mindfulness meditation is a tool we can use to train our brains to be more present in each moment of our lives — that includes basketball and <u>perceived</u> pressure situations. When we truly become mindful, there isn't a difference between the mindful player and the mindful person. They become one.

Stop Turning the Ball Over

Our brain processes thoughts and words as images. If you close your mind and imagine "basketball" you don't see words. You maybe see the ball, players, or some action throughout the course of the game. If we tell someone to "stop turning the ball over" the first thing that is going to be visualized is the thing we don't want them to do — turning the ball over. If you yell at a player to "stop fouling" the first thing that goes into his mind is an image of a foul.

Our brain processes those images, the images influence how we feel, how we feel influences how we act, how we act creates habits, and habits create change or improvements.

So if we want our players to "stop thinking and just play the game," we have to put images in their mind of what we want them to do — NOT what we DON'T want them to do. Yes, in certain circumstances we have to get people to understand what we do not want them to do. Because until they realize that the technique or process they are using is incorrect or not efficient, they will not be receptive to what is correct.

Ultimately though, what matters most is being completely dialed in on the task and focusing on the process for a consistent period of time. Mindfulness gives you the ability to tap into this.

Chapter 31
EVERYONE COMMUNICATES. FEW CONNECT.

"When I work with a writer, we share our own passionate and personal viewpoints, listen deeply and allow a third person to emerge with a new vision." -Wed Williamson, Art Director

With access to the Internet, the wealth basketball knowledge available today is incredible. And, if you take the time to learn, there's no better time to be a coach. But anyone can pick up some drills online and run a workout or practice. The real influencers understand that before anything else, you need to build a relationship.

You need to be able to reach your players, get them to trust you, and show them you care if you want to be able to maximize your influence. And this holds true for anyone in a leadership position.

John Maxwell's book <u>Everyone Communicates. Few Connect</u>, really changed my perspective on this. "Connecting is the ability to identify with people and relate to them in a way that increases your influence." Forever I used to think of this as being fake or phony. I always thought, "I'm not going to change who I am just so I can get someone else to listen to me."

Connect by giving them your complete attention. The eyes are the windows to the heart and soul.

People can feel if you care just by how you greet them, which I call 'The Kevin Eastman Effect.' Kevin Eastman is the Vice President of Basketball Operations for the Los Angeles Clippers and is a huge influencer in the basketball world. Here's part of the reason why: I've met him 3 or 4 times in the past few years, and while I'm sure he has no clue who I am, he's always has treated me like I'm his long lost best friend. His energy shows he cares because I think he truly does.

In the elite basketball programs the best players are always the hardest workers. And, that is a really difficult culture to create. Usually the players with the most athletic ability are always being told how great they are, which makes developing relationships with them even more important. If you aren't challenging your best player, and he's not setting an example of how to persist through adversity, it's going to be tough to get everyone else to. They are the bridge between you, the values you want to instill, and the rest of the team.

Here are some specific things I've come up with that will help you communicate, connect and challenge your players, ultimately developing a greater influence.

1-on-1 After Practice

If you are still in playing shape and can compete with your players, this might be one of the most powerful ways to develop a relationship with players. The competition creates a bond.

Defend During Drills

Players love coaches who will get out on the floor and sweat with them. It shows that you are invested by putting the work in just like they are. Play defense during drills that are typical 1 vs 0. This is a great way to get them quality reps as well.

Shooting Competition

Celtic Threes — The passer/rebounder is under the basket with the ball and the shooter starts in the corner three spot. The goal of the drill is to make 2 threes in a row from the corner, wing, top of the key, wing, and corner. Once you get to the opposite corner the drill starts again and you have to make your way back to where you started. The goal is to finish the drill in under 2 minutes. To make it competitive, see who can finish the drill in the shortest amount of time.

Celtic Mid-Range — This is similar to Celtic Threes except we start in the short corner and go to the elbow, free throw line, elbow, and opposite short corner. Since this is only 15 feet our goal is to try and finish the drill in 90 seconds.

Free Throw Contest

Free Throw Golf — I learned this from Dave MacArthur. It's a simple free throw competition that rewards you for not only makes, but swishes as well. We play 2 shots per round and usually 10 rounds.

Swish = (-1)

Make = (+0)

Miss = (+1)

Your goal after 10 rounds (20 shots) is to end up with the lowest score possible. Put a wager on the game — pushups or some sprints. You have no idea what type of power doing something as simple as this might be. It shows that you are invested in the player and in the program. I'll sometimes make a mistake demonstrating a drill at an event or workout. And when I recognize it I'll knock out some basketball pushups to show that I own my mistakes. You have to ask yourself if you're willing to invest as much as your players? And if you are find ways to physically demonstrate that.

Watching Game Film

Studying game film is one of the most underrated things players can do to improve their game. In addition to watching your own games, it's crucial to study other players of similar skill sets and athletic ability. If you really pay attention, the best players in the NBA are always stealing things from each other.

The best way to do this is in a small group or individually – just like you would run an individual instruction session. There are a few ways to do this.

1) Clip out segments of a game(s) of your players making mistakes, as well as, positive plays. Let the clips run, pause and rewind to stop and go more in depth explaining what you're expecting them to do.

2) Do the same thing except for use clips of a player with

similar skill sets and athletic ability.

3)   If you really want to get your players thinking, have them watch the entire game film with you, except, this time, give them the remote. When something happens make them stop, explain and teach you what they did right or did wrong. When you get them to think on your level this is when you will really make strides.

Tutoring

Maybe you have a player who is struggling in a certain class. While many schools probably have tutors or access to teachers, tutoring your players shows that you are invested in them not just as a player, but as a person. It also tells them "education is important" without having to actually say it.

Take Them Out To Eat

Everyone has to eat. Offer to take them home after practice and stop by Chipotle. Conversation naturally happens over food unless it's some awkward blind date.

Find Their Hot Button

Find out what they are interested in and what they care about outside of basketball. One of my mentors, Bill Peterson, was an Assistant Coach at Louisiana Tech, when they had a player with tremendous talent and potential, but wasn't putting in the time to see this come to life. Coach Peterson was always trying to find ways to get him to spend extra time individually with him in the gym. So he started asking around, trying to find out what this player was interested in outside of basketball. He found out that this player absolutely loved cars and loved to put them together.

So he scraped together some money (I'm sure LA Tech assistants at that time were getting paid today's Kentucky salary) and found an old car that this player could put together. He stopped over at this player's house from time to time to check in on how the car was progressing and eventually they started to build a relationship. Coach Peterson found his "hot button" something to connect with him on and to show him he really cared for him outside of basketball. They started to work out more, he started to work harder and eventually that player turned into one of the best Power Forwards in NBA History, Karl Malone.

Articles or Books

One of the greatest gifts you can give is the opportunity for someone to invest in themselves through reading. This is a great way to paint a picture for them of the work and sacrifice it takes to be great. When it was more relevant, I used to give players an article on Jason Terry transforming his game at Arizona after his freshman year by making 700 shots at 7 a.m. each day during the summer.

I've purchased Mind Gym, by Gary Mack, for countless players that they still have today. Or it might be recommending an App like HeadSpace that teaches guided meditation.

Simply Ask

Remember when I said the first step is to just simply care more? You need to demonstrate it. Talking to most teenagers this is going to be a "no, I'm fine," most of the time. Especially at the beginning of a relationship, but the more they get to know you, trust you, and like you, the more they will open up. The more they will allow you to help them out. Key point: follow through! Nothing kills influence and trust more than not following through on something they thought you were going to show up for.

Remember you don't want to just communicate with your players you need to find ways to connect. Being mindful of their hopes, dreams, and aspirations gives you a much better ability to connect and create a relationship. You can't teach them unless you can reach them and show them you truly care.

Learned Helplessness

Because we might have been introduced to something too early, had someone not believe in us, or simply didn't work hard enough at something, we can develop what is called 'Learned Helplessness.' This is when someone when someone doesn't try to get out of or work through a negative or uncomfortable situation because the past has taught them that they are helpless. And worse, so many people start to "over learn" learned helplessness and they apply it to all the situations in their life.

So a player who is learning some ball handling drills and really struggles with them can quickly start to believe that no matter how hard they work, they won't be able to improve. This is why it is crucial, no matter what level players are at, need to be training in their "Sweet Spot."

Studies show that when people actually believe that they can achieve something or attain a certain skill they work much harder. If you are sick of your people not working hard enough, maybe it's that they don't believe they can actually do what you are asking. When players are struggling through drills, I see disappointment in their body language that's telling me, "I'm never going to get this." I always counter with, "I'd never ask you to do something I didn't believe you could do." I'm not sure where I got that from, but it seems to really help players push through discomfort.

I've found that the best way to do this is simply showing them you care.... That you care about them as a person, and about their hopes, dreams, and aspirations. In order to do this really well you have to be extremely mindful of certain things that a player does. Paying attention to their body language is huge. You can tell so much about a player just by watching how he reacts when a teammate or coach says something to him, when he misses a shot, turns the ball over, or forgets a set that you are trying to run.

Here are a few things to look for:

- When you're in practice, or in the locker room, are you aware of how the players are or aren't interacting?

- Are your two best players never at the same basket during shooting drills or partners during passing?

- Do they both have a crush on the same girl?

- Do your players eat lunch together at school?

- Is your scout team getting sick of putting in tremendous effort everyday to get the team better, but never receiving any recognition from it?

You also have to be extremely mindful of your own body language when trying to connect with your kids. Does your body language contradict the words that come out of your mouth? Do you hang your head when your point guard turns the ball over, but tell him, "It's okay. Run it again." Is that really the best way to instill confidence in him?

Chapter 32
WHY SOCIAL MEDIA MIGHT BE KILLING YOUR DREAMS

Each morning I used to wake up, turn on my phone and check my social media. I'd do this before anything else because it was the easiest thing for me to do to try and feel connected. I had FOMO. Fear Of Missing Out. The thing I didn't realize was this led to me reacting to things right away in the morning. Things that were not working towards my highest area of contribution. In the mornings we are the most refreshed and have the most in our mental tank to be creative and tackle dough decisions. Studies have shown we truly do have a limited supply of will power, which is determined by how much sleep we get, how we fuel our body, and how we refresh ourselves through exercises, play and activities. Even more shocking, according to Dan Ariely, professor of Psychology and Behavioral Economics at Duke University, says most people only have 2 really productive hours in their day. Two hours!

And, maybe even worse, before I started checking social media in the mornings, what I used to do was wake up and check my email. I'd respond to everything that was urgent — not focusing on the overall vision and things I needed to do, investments I needed to make to get from where I was to where I wanted to be. Why?

Because it's doing little things, that **emotionally give us a sense of gratification**, which we want to do right away. Because it'll help us feel as if we've gotten something accomplished.

"When it comes to the pleasure of getting things done, people are like rats, repeatedly pressing a bar because it simulates their reward centers." - Inc. Magazine

This is exactly how we feel when we do things like check social media:

1) Check Twitter, Instagram, Facebook, or Snapchat

2) Feel good because we know what's going on

3) Like, Share, or Comment on something to make us feel connected

But in the big picture we aren't moving towards our vision.

Until I started yoga and meditation I wasn't even conscious of the fact the first thing I'd do each morning was check social media, and, how it was affecting my days. I'd see another basketball training company post new video and think to myself "we need to get a new video out" or someone posted a new blog and think that I, "had to write a blog today." I was starting my day reacting instead of intentionally putting my effort towards my ONE thing.

You might be waking up in the mornings — checking Twitter, Instagram, Facebook, and Snapchat — finding out what everyone else is doing. But, what we are doing here is searching for, hoping, to find something that makes us feel good. Something that makes us feel connected or maybe something that motivates us. You might be looking for the weather or to see who won the game last night, but these things are all out of your control. And, they aren't using your most productive hours towards your dreams.

When we start our day with things outside of our control, we react. When we start with things within our control we take intentional action.

Darren Hardy has a strategy that he calls "Bookending" your days. The first thing he does in the morning and the last thing he does at night is always within his control. You never know what is going to show up during the middle of your day, what fires you might have to put out, or people that need to talk to you that day. But you can start your day off with the things that you need to get done to put yourself in a position to have a successful day — whether that's meditation, exercise, or reading — you're in control. What you do before you go to sleep at night is also within your control.

And, it can also get out of control — for me I got into the bad habit of watching Netflix shows before I went to sleep. My excuse was that whatever I read at night was always related to work and Netflix was my one time throughout the day to actually not work. But, the worst thing about this was that it significantly cut into my reading time. I used to read each night until I was tired enough to go to sleep — usually between 45-60 minutes. Not only did I sleep better when reading I almost always was going to bed earlier. And studies show that what you read at night can have a big impact on your morning.

Once I realized I wasn't reading (one of my principles), and my sleep was being affected, I moved my phone into another room and now use something else for an alarm. If I wasn't mindful of how I was feeling, how it was affecting me personally, and how it was affecting my work, who knows when or if I would have changed.

I think all of us get caught up in little things like this throughout our day that we aren't even aware of. Things that might seem small and insignificant when added up, really start to affect our mind. And, unless we become more aware of our thoughts, feelings, and actions we won't know what's affecting us. We won't know if we have something we can change or improve. Now that I've moved my phone into another room, something very small and seemingly insignificant, when I wake up I'm focused on what I need to do to start my day off right.

But it's the awareness created through mindfulness meditation that gave me the ability to change.

I'm sure for me there are things that I'm not even aware of yet, that have been going on for years, which I'll change when I create more awareness. So now instead of reacting to social media, email, and other things outside of my control, through mindfulness meditation I'm able to create a little mental space. And this mental space helps you detach so you start to reflect and respond in intentional ways. Intentional actions that will move you towards your dreams.

Chapter 33
PLAY PRESENT

Great players never get too high or too low. They play with a consistent level of energy and emotion. It's the same for leaders, teachers, or anyone in a high-pressure position.

They don't let themselves get wrapped up in the emotions of the game or project, where they don't play by their instincts, and start to view the situation as pressure instead of an opportunity. When you get wrapped up in emotions, either high or low, it lowers your ability to stay present and focus on the process. Whether it's a bad call, a turnover, or getting pulled out of the game you have to be able to come back to the present. Center your mind and focus on the things you can control.

Imagine being a player in a huddle where your coach decides to take an aggressive tone. He wants to challenge the team and instill a sense of urgency. As you approach the huddle you see his intensity and immediately start thinking "Man, here we go again. He's going to yell at us." Soon enough as he is drawing up the next strategy your mind wanders...

"Dude is drawing so hard on the clipboard, could he just chill out for once?"

He finishes the talk and the huddle is about to break. You're thinking, "Thank goodness that's over." Immediately followed by, "Wait. What's that play he drew up?"

In this scenario you're attention fixated on one component of a larger picture. Yes, perhaps your coach's body language and tone were abrasive. But maybe that was his intent. To instill that urgency and get some energy back into the team. That being so, you have allowed his portrayal of emotion to deter you from your responsibilities as a player in that huddle, on that team, in that game. You've compromised your team's chances of winning the next play and potentially the game.

And for what?

Because your coach drew on the board too hard with the marker.

Let's flip the situation. You're a coach, down by 1 with 13 seconds left ,and just called a timeout. Do you take a deep breath and in a calm, collected demeanor explain to your kids what you want them to do? When I was coaching there was a direct correlation to how well our guys executed and my demeanor in a time out.

Don't get it twisted — a team is a reflection of their coach. If you're feeding them intense and anxious energy how do you expect them to go out on the floor, calm, cool, and collected — ready to execute.

Your players can little feel your energy and will perform accordingly.

In either case, practicing meditation gives us the ability to carry out this focused, calm and relaxed demeanor into the rest of our day. And when I say calm, I don't mean low energy. It's a combination of calm and energy at the same time, which is tough to explain until you experience it. At its core meditation is training your mind behave the way you want it to in daily life. In practice, work, and school. So when your coach draws too hard on the clip board, someone tells you your project needs a lot more work, or you have the ball in your hands with 9 seconds left down by 1, you can stay completely present. You don't take things personally and see these are just things that are happening. They don't determine your worth as a human being. And, instead of being lost, trying to protect your ego, you're completely focused on the task at hand.

A big reason coaches, players, and leaders get so high and to low is that we place so much emphasis on winning. When this happens we lose focus of the things that actually determine whether or not we win. And focusing on the process is actually the only thing that we can control. We can only control the work we put in, not the fruits of our labor. As Phil Jackson says, "We only control the work. Not the rings."

Without meditation you can't reach the type of awareness that I've discussed above, but these concepts below are a great first step. The concept "Play Present" from sports psychologist Graham Betchardt can be simplified as focusing on one task at a time throughout the game.

Below are a few phrases we use that in basketball (and life) that are situation specific to help us and our players "Play Present."

It's 4 concepts or teaching points that you can use to help you stay mindful and play present during practices or games.

"One for One"

It's amazing how difficult it is to stay focused throughout a workout — great players have **developed** ability to do this. We use this phrase 'One for One' in every shooting drill that we do. It helps players focus on shooting one shot at a time, not thinking about the last shot they missed or the one 30 seconds in the future that they are trying to make. Focus on your feet and your follow through, one shot at a time — every time. We don't want to just get up 500 shots. We want to shoot 1 shot 500 times.

"Next Play"

This concept is from Duke Basketball and Coach K. I think this phrase is appropriate for after a mistake is made. Mistakes are part of the game and life — expect them, accept them, and move on. So many times 1 mistake leads another mistake or a lack of focus on the next possession. By using the phrase "Next Play," we are turning our attention and focus immediately to the next thing in our control.

"1-0"

Preparing for a game the only thing we want players to focus on is the one ahead of us. Every game is a big game and needs to be treated that way. Specifically here we want to focus on the process of going "1-0" – things we can control like rebounding, spacing the floor, closing out, and communicating.

"1 Stop"

Defensively if you can focus on getting one stop at a time throughout a game you are going to be successful. It's extremely difficult to focus all your effort on one single defensive possession at a time, and the teams that do, reap the benefits. Closeout, contain, and contest. Rebound — it's not a stop until you do. To challenge your team see how many stops you can get in a row. Keep adding them up. Set records and beat records.

If you can discipline yourself to be present — yes it's a choice — with your feet on every shot, making each dribble move quicker and maximum effort on every possession you'll have more enjoyment from the game, and make quicker improvements.

"My heroes growing up, the Jordans, the Bill Russells, the Magic Johnsons, they all won multiple times. I wanted more. But it wasn't just the result. It was the journey to get there...I love the process. The results come later." - Kobe Bryant

We need deep, deliberate practice to improve, and "Playing Present" is how you get there.

Chapter 34
WHAT SUCCESS IS DISGUISED AS

When Barack Obama was running for election, Russell Simmons, a huge meditation and mindfulness advocate, put a ton of time on working to make sure the hip-hop community got out to vote and support Obama. The night of the election at a party, when it looked Obama was going to win, everyone started popping champagne and celebrating. Russell decided to duck out early. It's not that he wasn't happy Obama won. So why did he do it?

"Because a constant contentment is what I'm looking for. I'm more interested in feeling balanced and peaceful all of the time, not just when something 'good' is happening." - Russell Simmons

The more I learn about myself this is exactly what I'm seeking — inner peace.

And, I think deep down everyone else is as well. I have been so focused on the end result that I haven't enjoyed the journey, done the work and let go of the outcome. The truth is, there really is only so much you can control. When you're always focused on the end result like earning a scholarship, getting that new car, or latest sneaker release, you're taking your mind out of the present. And the present is the only place you can get into that flow state and feel that sense of inner peace. Because in the end, that is what every single one of our actions is intended to do. Make us happy.

Contrary to popular belief, success does not lead to happiness.

Ironically, "inner peace," is essentially the definition of success from the one of the greatest coaches in sports history.

"Success is a peace of mind which is a direct result of self-satisfaction in knowing you did your best to become the best you are capable of becoming." - John Wooden

I do believe this is truly the best definition of success, yet is the hardest to instill in yourself, and the people you are trying to lead: your players, co-workers, children, teammates, or students. The most difficult part is getting them to realize what it truly means to try their hardest. Not just at the moment of competition, but equally as important in preparation. Until you can truly look at yourself and say that you tried your best, you will never be able to feel the "peace of mind" that comes with success. I think the main reason people define success by objective goals is because it is much easier to do. It's much easier to just look at the scoreboard rather than reflect on your efforts and preparation in attaining a specific goal.

The flip side of this definition is being able to accept the fact that you did truly give your best effort and know that there is nothing else you could have done. Your performance cannot affect your self-esteem and how you feel about yourself.

"The pursuit of happiness becomes the biggest source of our unhappiness."- Dan Harris

I've got a car I never thought I'd have, live where people take vacation, have built a business many people dream about, and worked the top 1% of the basketball players in the world. But none of these things in and of themselves will make you happy.

You're not chasing these things. You're chasing the feeling that you think they are going to give you when you get them. And through meditation you can find that feeling right now. It exists within you.

Chapter 35
A BEGINNER'S MIND

A big concept in Buddhism is to practice having a "beginner's mind." Each breath, each posture, each movement you want to practice it like it is the first time you have ever done it. Why? So you are present in each breath you take and move you make. Being present is the ultimate level of focus and concentration. And if we can use mediation and yoga to train our minds to be present this becomes a powerful habit. When we have to schedule things and have constant reminders — those things are hard. But, when we have habits, they are easy. I'm not talking about walking around in this zombie-like state of mind. Rather the opposite - focusing on each detail as it's practiced.

In Daniel Coyle's book <u>The Talent Code,</u> he breaks down what it truly takes to develop your innate talents.

The first element of developing talent is Deep Practice, which requires tremendous awareness and focus. The problem is that 'practice' is a relative term, like hard work. Let's define it.

THREE RULES OF DEEP PRACTICE

Chunk it up – Whole Part Method

1. Explain

2. Demonstrate

3. Repetition

4. Correct

5. Repeat

6. Compete

Repeat It: Find The Sweet Spot For Repetition

1. Conventional practices states that shooting 500 jumpers is better than shooting 250 jumpers. Spending more time is only effective if you are still in the sweet spot, at the edge of your capabilities, building and honing your circuits.

2. Kevin Eastman, Vice President of Basketball Operations for the Los Angeles Clippers and Nike Skills Academy Director says this about workouts: Two things that will kill your workouts are fatigue and boredom. You need to find ways to eliminate these.

Slow It Down To Be Able To Feel The Correct Form.

I had a chance to watch Steve Nash go through a short pre-game workout against the Milwaukee Bucks. He started in close at about 5 feet, going far less than game speed, working on having a perfect release – feeling perfect form. Even as he moved out working on a series of step backs and pull-ups everything was done slowly, focusing on perfect footwork and release. His feet were <u>exactly the same</u> on every shot and he didn't move on to the next move until he made 5 shots from each spot. This is so much more about deep focus and the <u>feel</u> of perfection instead of going game speed.

Traditional theories of "game speed, game speed!" are contradicted here. Instead of getting players to "go hard" all of the time we need to teach them to "feel perfection." I always use the analogy at camps that if you are going 100 mph doing a drill the wrong way, it doesn't matter how hard you go, you aren't going to get better.

You need form first — technique first — then speed. And the awareness to know the difference.

If you don't know why focus is huge, Tony Fryer explains it here:

"The part of psychology most relevant to sports performance is neuroscience. A major concept of neuroscience is that everything you do is controlled by thought. Your body is controlled by your mind. Controlling your mind through thought is called focus.

"Peak performance requires focus. You must have very specific purpose and intent. Simplify that purpose to the smallest variable possible, and that becomes your focal point. You don't need to think, but you do need to focus! Pure focus equals maximum performance!" - Tony Fryer (USAB article)

Practicing mindfulness keeps you at a beginner's mind, being present, and always taking the first step. It allows you to more regularly be in this state of deep practice and wrapping myelin, the stringy white stuff in our brain that creates muscle memory. And the more myelin we wrap the more habit we create.

Chapter 36

ARE YOU INTERESTED OR COMMITTED?

Mindfulness gives you the ability to see whether you are really committed to something, really in love with something, or if you are just interested. So many times we are putting forth effort into something we don't truly love to do. But, we have to be able to see the difference if we really want to be happy.

And, you must understand that even if you are in love with something, you aren't going to feel like doing it all the time. That's why it's called commitment.

My parents had been on me for years to do more than just work. They knew I worked all the time and didn't make much time for social things or other activities. I really enjoyed working, reading, working out, cooking, and of course basketball. But other than that, I didn't do a lot of the typical things that make most people happy: trips, going to movies, shows, concerts, camping, etc. I read a mantra in Elizabeth Gilbert's book, The Happiness Project, "Do what makes you happy. Not what's supposed to make you happy."

But, one thing I had always loved was dogs. We had them growing up, my roommate had one before I moved to Milwaukee and just had never thought I'd have enough time to take care of one on my own with my work schedule and travel. Like several things in my life, I finally just decided to pull the trigger and figure it out along the way. If you really want something, most of the time you'll figure out a way to make it work. And so, in 2011, a little princess named entered my life.

This was one of the best decisions I ever made in my life, but it wasn't all flowers and unicorns. So the story I tell at our events, goes like this...

"How many of you have a pet at home — A dog, cat, or other animal?" I ask and most of the kids raise their hands.

How many of you would say that you absolutely, 100%, love your pet like it's part of your family?" and all of the hands stay up.

I continue: "I got a dog 4 years ago and she is the love of my life. One of the best decisions I've ever made. But, do you think when I've been on the road and don't get home until 1 a.m., that when she was a puppy, whining and crying to get up and go outside at 6 a.m., that I loved waking up, putting on clothes, and taking her outside? Especially if this was in the middle of a freezing cold, Wisconsin winter? Of course not. But, I when I got her I made a commitment to love her, care for her, and protect her."

So there are going to be times, many times, when you love something, when you're committed to something and you don't feel like doing it. There are going to be times when you have to make sacrifices. When you have to get up at 6 a.m. and lift before school, or stay up late working on a school project because you had a game on the road that night.

What would happen to that pet you love if you only walked them when YOU felt like it? Played with them when YOU felt like it? Or gave them food and water when YOU felt like it? They would get sick, weak, and maybe even die.

That's exactly what happens to your game or whatever else it is that you are committed to. Your game will get sick, weak and maybe even die. If you're in love, truly in love, there are going to be times when you don't feel like doing the work. But you know that the benefits greatly outweigh the work and learn to find the joy in the process. It's just about changing your mindset.

I could either focus my attention on how cold it was at 6 a.m. taking Peyton outside in the snow, or I could focus how ridiculously adorable it was watching her play in the snow. You can focus on how everyone else is still sleep, or you can focus on how you are getting ahead. You can only be focused on one thing at once — see it as a challenge and process of growth as a player and person.

It's about what you choose to focus on and what you focus on will expand.

Chapter 37

I WAS A PAPER BOY.
AND, WHY THAT MATTERS.

From age 11 to 13, I had a paper route. It was one of the greatest experiences I could have had as kid that had nothing to do with basketball. Though I didn't know it at the time, essentially it was like running your own business. If I screwed up — didn't deliver someone their paper, their paper was wet from the snow, or I was late making the delivery deadline — I had to deal with it. It was my responsibility to make it right. And, back then, it was a big deal if you missed your newspaper. You couldn't just hop online and see what was going on in the world.

All this responsibility taught me leadership.

Leadership

Coaches have complained to me how they don't have any leaders on the team this year. My question to them is: what are you doing to develop your leaders? Are you putting them in a position to develop the leadership skills that you want to see?

Leaders are NOT born. Leaders are nurtured, molded, and taught. This is why we try to train our kids to become not only good basketball players but to assume leadership.

How do we do this?

Embracing Failure

Kids need to learn to deal with failure. Failing and learning to bounce back is an essential quality for leadership. Kids learn that mistakes are learning opportunities. They are opportunities to grow.

The problem is though, as coaches, teachers, and leaders, we don't put kids in a position often enough where they can feel uncomfortable and fail. By giving them some level of responsibility when they are younger — even small responsibilities — we provide them an opportunity to learn to deal with mistakes, even if trivial, and therefore with failure. Only by doing this can they learn to transcend failure, grow, and improve so they could better actualize their potential.

Awareness Of Strengths

A big part of developing leaders is having the awareness to know what your people are already good at, putting them in a position to be successful, and using the confidence they build from that situation as a stepping stone to the next level. Being mindful about what tasks and projects you assign your team, as well as what their strengths are will help you move more efficiently towards the vision of the organization.

GET OUT OF THE WAY

A couple years ago we started having some of our older players lead the first part of workouts. Usually this was some ball handling drills or a dribbling dynamic warm-up they had been doing for years. Some of them absolutely hated it. And, some were almost embarrassed that they could crush some of these drills. But, it put them in a position where they had to speak and had to lead in something they were already highly skilled in.

We saw this developing leadership carry over into different parts of the workouts. For example, some of the players, while in line waiting for their next rep, would watch a younger player go through their finish at the rim. When the younger player got back in line, the older ones would show them some teaching points that would help them perform the move better. As a leader you have to take your ego out of it. If I was a middle school player I'd much rather learn from a college or high school kid than my coach. It's the "cool" factor.

This proved to be win-win: by teaching, the older players understood the skills on a much deeper level. By being coached, the younger players got the attention and help from someone they looked up to. Imagine how they felt that an older player, maybe even a NCAA D1 or NBA player took the time to show them that they care, changing the trajectory of their day, maybe even life. This all started because we put someone in a position of possibly making a mistake. By allowing them this discomfort, they transformed into leaders. They grew.

Ways you can start developing leadership:

- Leading stretching

- Leading warm-ups and ball handling

- Breaking down a film session

- Coaching younger kids

After many attempts to teach kids leadership skills, we came up with 4 different levels of trust that you can delegate to your team. Progressing sequentially through these levels, which increases in responsibility helps them manage best, just as they build up going from 1-ball stationary to 2-ball stationary drills.

Level I. Singular tasks such as sweeping the gym floor, making a copy of an article, calling a client back, or grabbing 4 cones for the workout. Simple lists of tasks that need to simply get done.

Level II. Having a specific measurable goal that needs to be reached where you as a leader are providing direction and oversight.

Level III. Having a specific measurable goal or project assigned where you are not providing direction or oversight. The player, assistant coach or employee is completely responsible for accomplishing the task. You are just providing the goal.

Level IV. An employee, assistant coach, or player does something on his or her own, without your direction, to positively impact the mission of the organization. You are trusting their insight and understanding of the organization's mission to best use their time.

You need to have a mix of all 4, but getting more of your people to Level IV is the highest level of trust.

It helps to have an understanding of these levels, especially when delegating tasks or trying to build trust within your team. You can't expect new players, coaches, or employees to join your team and be able to handle Level IV Trust without moving through Levels I, II, and III first.

A big part of developing leaders is having the awareness to

know what your people are already good at, putting them in a position to be successful, and using the confidence they build from that situation as a stepping stone to the next level. Being mindful about what tasks and projects your assigning to your team, as well as, what their strengths are, will help you move more efficiently towards the vision of the organization.

Chapter 38
THE INVESTMENT

Bob Knight said basketball is 80% mental and 20% physical. No matter what you think the percentage is there is definitely a relationship.

When we ask coaches and players if they think sports and life are at least a portion 'mental,' everyone raises their hand. If we ask if it's over 50% mental, many hands go up. How much time do we spend training our mind? The answer for most of us is — very little. Why not?

One reason is that many people don't know where to start and so they procrastinate. It's the same with someone trying to improve their basketball shooting form or golf swing. Things that make us uncomfortable we tend to put off or neglect to do altogether. Or we just assume that it's a natural by-product of competitive sports. While there is some truth to that the reality is that it's a practice. Something that has to be cultivated.

Two of the greatest basketball players ever — Michael Jordan and Kobe Bryant — both intentionally trained their mind, body, and skill. They both practiced meditation and different forms of visualization. Until you are focusing on all three of these, you cannot truly reach your full potential in anything that you do.

Exercise for Every Body

Training your body is important for everyone, not just those in Crossfit, training like an NBA player, or running marathons.

Most people feel so crappy from lack of exercise and nutrition that they don't know how good their body is supposed to feel.

Research has revealed many holistic benefits from moving your body strenuously to new limits.

- Provides a natural high releasing endorphins in your body and balancing neurotransmitters like serotonin, the feel good hormone, and dopamine, our reward hormone.

- Serves as an anti-depressant as well as Prozac.

- Improves memory and cognitive function.

- Boosts confidence.

- Improves sleep.

- Relieves stress.

- Taps into creativity.

There is a correlation between pushing your body and

pushing your mind. Mental toughness is built from physically pushing yourself to the point you think you can't go any further. Then pushing yourself some more. It's the effort after you think you've done your best that counts the most. That's the one that builds mental toughness and character.

Now, I'm not suggesting that if you're working on your game for 12 hours during the week, you spend 4 hours on skills, 4 hours on your body, and 4 hours on your mind. You have to spend the time in proportion to what you need in order to get the results that you want. But the great thing about working on your mind, is that you are really also training for life.

Physical toughness and mental skills are also built from mentally pushing yourself past the limit you think your body can't go any further. Can't do that last set of squats or run that last flight of stairs? Your body will give up way sooner than your mind. Practice inspiring self-talk. You can be your own best motivator. If you can push your mind, you can push your body.

Mind Power

Working on your mind is an investment in your game and your life and a lifelong endeavor. And, like skill development or strength training, it takes time to see serious results. You have to mentally prepare yourself for times where you will plateau and times where you will dip.

If you're just starting out playing the game and spend 10 hours a week for a month, you are going to improve at a significantly higher rate than someone who is in the NBA. Those 10 hours per week, might just be needed to maintain where he is at.

It's the same with strength and conditioning, which I'm sure a lot of you have experienced. When you first start a consistent strength and conditioning program, the results in the beginning are great. There is a pretty short "improvement curve" where you start to see changes in your conditioning, movements, and strength.

It's talked about much more in lifting, but there can be plateaus in everything we do. The best find ways to make changes and adapt their training in order to keep improving. The crazy thing about training your mind is that it doesn't stop. You can ALWAYS improve. Like golf, it's a life-long activity. In lifting, you are going to reach a point where you need to just maintain where you are at. Basketball players don't want to look like football players. It's counter productive to your game.

For coaches, it's like investing in skill development over X's and O's and plays. When your players have the skills to pass, pivot, and handle the basketball, it doesn't matter what offense you run. You can run whatever you think fits best for the skill set of the players you have. If you focus on sets and X's and O's, there is a point where you continually have to make changes.

It's way easier to prepare for and scout a great offense than it is to scout against great players.

So at the beginning, you probably are going to see results quickly. Then it will plateau a bit, and you have to consistently work on it to continue to see small improvements over time. This is the

'Compound Effect' I discussed earlier, where your daily, consistent, practices, and habits will come to fruition.

10,000 Hours

"The 10,000 Hour Rule," made popular by Malcolm Gladwell, is a great example of investing in your mind. It's like writing this book. Doing a small part, each day, will add up over the long run.

It's not something that you can just do once in a while. If you train your mind once in a while, you'll have once in a while results. The overnight celebrity knows better than anyone he didn't become a celebrity overnight. It's about being prepared for, and aware of, opportunities that present themselves to you. Yeah, you might get your 15 minutes of fame, but that's not an authentic representation of your efforts and actions to realize your potential.

So start now. Start small. It's the daily investments that will change the course of your life.

Chapter 39
WHY YOU SHOULD JUMP OFF A CLIFF

I went on my first yoga retreat in Hana, a very underdeveloped part of Maui, which didn't even have paved roads until the 1990's. I learned so much about myself by going completely offline, focusing on myself, and serving others who were there. It was the most epic, adventurous, and life-changing week of my life. But, as much as I learned from myself, I learned just as much from a scared, lost, and frightened girl from Jersey. Laurel had just got out of a serious relationship, looking to change careers after 8 years, and possibly move across the country.

Throughout the week every one of the 16 people at the retreat jumped off a 35-foot cliff into the Venus pools in Maui. Day by day, each person got a little more courage to jump off. And by the last day the only person who had not jumped off was Laurel. She kept saying "It's not that I'm afraid. I just have no desire."

Deep down, our fears kill our wildest desires and dreams.

So on the last day, about an hour before we were supposed to head back to the airport, I grabbed her phone and started walking to the cliff — knowing she'd follow her phone. I asked her, "When have you ever done anything worthwhile in your life that you weren't a little afraid of or wasn't hard to do?" She thought about it for a second and answered, "Nothing."

Joe, a guy from Brooklyn, got her off the couch and started walking after me, with words of encouragement. When we finally got to the cliff, she was terrified. Almost shaking. But, it wasn't the actually risk she feared. It was her perception of the risk. Humans aren't supposed to jump off cliffs 35 feet high. We forget that there is water below.

When you first jump off the cliff, it's not about jumping for the fun of it.

It's about jumping off the cliff in spite of the fear. It's about training your mind to be uncomfortable in a situation of perceived risk.

Emphasis on <u>perceived</u>. And once you become more mindful you realize so many of our fears are perception. They aren't reality. But many times, because we don't have the ability to detach emotionally, these stories of fear and failure get looped in our head. Even though they are nothing close to the truth.

So when we choose to face these perceived fears over and over again, we start to believe so much more is possible in our lives. Even if we fail, we view them as a learning experience. An opportunity to grow and use it as a springboard for other areas of our life. For Laurel it wasn't about jumping off the cliff. It's about training her mind to know she CAN switch careers, move across the country, and embrace a new relationship with an open heart.

So jump off your cliff.

Trust yourself.

There is always water.

Chapter 40

EVERYBODY DIES. BUT NOT EVERYBODY LIVES.

I'm not really sure how to start, so let's just get straight to the point.

You will, eventually, die.

Your next breath might be your last, and tonight may very well be the last time you ever go to sleep. Nothing is guaranteed. But, don't get me wrong. I'm not trying to scare you. I'm trying to provide you with a potentially powerful mind shift. Here's what I mean:

In our western culture we are so afraid of death that we never talk about it, even though it's the only thing really guaranteed in life. And, contrary to what we like to think, there really isn't a whole lot we can do about it. But, what we can do, is change our perspective. Instead of hiding from it, we can change our relationship with it, and view it as our friend. View it as a constant reminder that this life will go by in a flash, and every second, of every minute, of every single day matters. Tremendously.

At about age 24, I was exposed to a really powerful exercise in a book, which I still process in my mind probably about once a month. And, while it's not specifically a mindfulness exercise it creates a crazy amount of awareness.

The exercise is to write out your own obituary as if you had died today.

That's some pretty intense stuff, right?

What would the people say about you? When you write this out you'll discover the things that, deep down, really matter to you. And, you'll also have a clear dashboard of where you actually spending your time. No one on their deathbed wishes they had accumulated more things, had a bigger house, and a nicer car. Is there anything inherently wrong with those? No. I'm all about living a life of abundance. But it's our relationship to those things that matters most. If you have a mansion, enjoy it. If you have a 1986 Buick LeSabre, enjoy it. Be present.

It's different for everyone, but when it comes to my obituary I really only care about 2 things:

1. The love I've shared
2. The impact I made

I want people to say, "He loved me, he truly cared, and inspired me to pursue my potential."

When you clarify what you want people to say about you when you die you get clarity on how you want to live your life. It gives you the ability to start making changes <u>right now</u> to live the life you would be proud of.

And, the great thing is that the things you think you might regret, you can start to change right now. Remember, without awareness we cannot change. For me, I never take time off. I'm constantly working, but I am finally starting to realize this is a real issue — both personally and professionally. It's an issue, not only with being able to recover and refresh, but to be able to live a life with no regrets. Eventually it starts to wear on you. In the first 9 years of my professional life I took off a total of 10 true days off. No phone and no computer.

But even though I am a believer that you can't be at your greatest on an empty fuel tank, it's something I haven't practiced. It's like trying to drive a Ferrari on fumes. You'll eventually crash and burn. So, recently, I made a conscious decision, that no matter the circumstances, I needed to take at least one trip per year like the retreat in Maui. I think travel does two things. It puts you in some uncomfortable situations (like extreme poverty I saw in Indonesia), and it increases empathy. And, by being in nature, in awe of some of the natural creations of the world, you are completely present. I think these two things have a way of resetting your system and balancing you out.

A couple quotes from two very unrelated people fit seamlessly with this idea:

"The more you become the more you can give." - Jim Rohn

"Unless you are selfish and put yourself first, you can't love yourself. You can't develop that love within yourself. And if you don't become love you can't give love." - An Indian spiritual guide named Osho

And recently I've come to realize the biggest part of becoming <u>more</u> is acceptance, self-care, self-compassion, and self-love. So without taking vacation, without taking time to love myself, I wasn't going to be able to live out the mission of my life. I wouldn't have the obituary I wanted.

So stop acting like you have all this time.

All this time to get better at your craft.

All this time to start that business.

All this time to do something you've dreamed about.

Start.

Now.

By making death our friend it helps us be truly present. To be completely aware and conscious in every single moment. When we realize this, instead of just attending events or buying things, we begin to experience them. And, we don't cling to the happiness because we know the only thing we can really do is be completely present in this current moment.

This awareness of death is a right hook that says, **"You don't have that much time. Be here now."**

So my closing challenge to you is this:

Write out that obituary. Be truthful, be vulnerable, and write from your heart. And then take that obituary, turn it into the mission of your life, and start living it out.

Every.

Single.

Day.

BOOK III

BRING YOU TO LIFE

Chapter 41

MY THREE DAILY QUESTIONS

Many times I get to the end of my day, take a shower after a workout, and start to think about whether or not I had a successful day. And, for so long, this was based on either emotional or outcome-based things like making a ton of progress on a project or signing a new client. I determined my success based on how I felt. But what I ultimately wanted to know was:

Did I do the best I possibly could that day to move towards my vision while keeping peace of mind?

When you break it down, that's what we are all searching for: a calm, present, and happy state of being.

Eventually I came up with three questions to ask to determine whether or not I had a successful day. They are all things that are conscious choices that I am in control of every single day.

Did I work towards my dreams? Not just the daily tasks that you need to get done. Did I do something that is part of my bigger dream. My mission in life. My ONE Thing task (if you're using the concept I mentioned earlier)? If you're blocking out time to pursue the big picture, the day-to-day things will eventually get done.

Did I do something for myself? Everyone who has been on an airplane has gone through the flight attendant demonstration explaining that you need to put on your air mask before assisting any children, partners, or pets. Why? Because if you don't take care of yourself first, you're not going to be able to help anyone else.

- Did you eat plant-based all day?

- Did you meditate?

- Did you get some exercise in?

For many people in a leadership position, this is a really tough concept to fully understand because they are so focused on serving. I probably struggle with this more than anything else, but the more mindful I become, the easier it gets.

Making a daily investment in yourself is making an investment in your ability to impact others.

Did I do something for someone else? I believe we are put here to do two things for others. Love and serve. Did you do something for someone else today to make his or her day a little easier? Or did you do something today to help someone work towards achieving their dreams? If you're in an occupation like a teacher or coach, you are doing this on a daily basis, but try to go above and beyond this. The extra little things like sending a student an article on a topic they might be passionate about.

If you want to look back on life and know that you mattered, don't <u>just</u> do the <u>required</u> work. Do the unrequired, impactful work.

I guarantee you that when you look back at these three questions, if you can answer yes, you'll sleep a lot better at night.

Chapter 42
HOW TO MAXIMIZE TEAM STRETCHING

In basketball it's crucial that we communicate. We have to communicate on help defense, guarding ball screens, and pin downs. But, as an individual we have to look inward. We have to look inward to grow. To become more aware of our thoughts, adjust them and be more centered in order to be more focused and play with more flow.

As a coach, the last thing you're probably looking for is one more thing you think you have to fit into practice. If that's you, I have a solution for you. Instead of having players count during stretching, have them silently count their breaths. Instead of holding a stretch and counting to 20, you can have them breathe together, in unison. By looking inward as a group there is something deeper that connects each individual to each other. This is something Phil Jackson used to do with the Bulls and Lakers. He also used to have them hold hands, which I have no idea how he got a group of grown ass men to do.

So if you are doing a static stretch you just have the players count their breaths like this:

You count "1" with the first inhale...

"2" with the exhale...All the way up to 20.

In order to keep everyone on the same page when you are stretching you will want to designate a leader who has the team switch when he gets to 20. He might be a couple breaths ahead or behind some of the rest of the group. But, when he gets to 20 he can direct them to switch to the next stretch.

Because the goal is not to have everyone end at "20" at the same time. Everyone has their own rhythm. Their own breath. The goal is for each member of the team to be focused on their breath. To look inward, quiet their mind start to become aware of their thoughts. Whether they are emotional, funny, or stressful, the goal is to be able to create more awareness. And once they start to sit with their thoughts, they start to detach from them and realize they are completely separate from their thoughts. For many, this will start to take away the power of their negative thinking patterns, which helps them be more present, more confident, and ultimately a better a player and person.

Eventually they will realize: "I am not my thoughts. I am an observer of my thoughts. I am the creator of my own experience. "

Chapter 43

STOP. SIT. BREATHE.

I understand it might be ridiculously out of your comfort zone to start meditating. Yes, it was originally practiced by yogis in India, but as you learned, it's a tool some of the highest achievers in the world have used to elevate their craft. Michael Jordan, Kobe Bryant, Steve Jobs, Phil Jackson. The list is crazy long. But, if you're not sold yet, here are some times throughout the day to start to become more mindful without having a full-on meditation session.

Literally all you need to do at any of these times is...

Stop.

Sit.

Breathe.

As you inhale, you'll count all the way up to five. When you get to the top of your breath, hold it for five seconds. Then, count backwards from five back down to one. Feel your stomach expand as you make your way up to five. Feel your stomach soften as you count down to one. It should help you come back to the present and become more aware of your thoughts.

If you need more time, or course, go longer. But remember, it's the quality, the focus on <u>each individual breath</u> that counts the most. Not the amount of time. You can even fit this in:

- Anytime you feel stress or anxiety come on

- When you get into your car

- Before you sit down to eat

- Tying shoes before practice

- When you wake up in the morning (even though I find this hard because I fall back asleep, but it works for some people)

- At the stoplight

- Dead ball

- Walk down the opposite side of the street you normally walk

- Drive a different route than you normally take to school or work

- When you get subbed out of the game

- When you check in at the scorer's table

- When the bell rings in between classes

- When you sit down for a meeting

- Before you take a test

- Walk through a door

- When you turn on your computer for the first time each day

A Few Tips On Breathing

1. Breathe through your stomach — not your chest. As an athlete, your body learns to breathe through your chest in order to engage your core while performing a physical activity. Unfortunately this is where stress and anxiety also live. When you were born, you naturally breathed through your stomach. Feel your ribs expanding out to the sides and stomach outward. Practicing this type of breathing will also help increase your lung capacity.

2. Don't force or try to control your breathing. When I first started meditating I tried to count and control every single breath I took. Fortunately one of my teachers corrected this and helped create a much deeper level of relaxation and calm. You are naturally going to breathe, so all you need to do is become aware of your breathing.

3. Get still. If our bodies are moving, it's really tough to silence our minds. When we push ourselves harder and we start to get fatigued, the first thing that starts to go is our thoughts. It's not our bodies. By stopping for 10-15 seconds between every drill (this might be a dead ball in a game), and taking a few deep, slow breaths, you're training your mind to reset. To refocus on the task, drill, or exercise you're performing next.

4. Breathe slow and feel the flow. Go as slow as possible and feel the air coming in through your nose... and out through your mouth. The mind follows your breath. The slower you breathe, so sooner your mind will calm down and put you back in the present.

Chapter 44

MYTHS AND CHALLENGES WITH MEDITATION

Are there going to be challenges with meditation? Of course, like with anything that you are trying to make improvements in, there are going to be peaks and valleys.

It Will Be Easy

Meditation is a mental discipline. It's training. It's like making a commitment to make 250 shots, drink a green juice, or exercise every day.

You Aren't Supposed To Think of Anything

Thoughts and emotions arising during meditation are completely normal. And, will be a part of it, no matter how hard you try. Once you start to recognize them, though, you can let them go and focus back on your breath. The longer you practice, the longer the gaps will be between thoughts and emotions.

You'll Instantly Feel a Zen-like Feeling of Calm and Peace

It's not going to happen. Just like you can't walk into a gym and instantly have Steph Curry handles, start dunking the ball, or spraying threes. It's an investment. But over time, you will see results. You will be calmer, make better decisions, be more mindful, and more compassionate.

Couldn't I Be Getting More Stuff Done?

This was by far my biggest challenge with mediation. And, to be honest, it still is. I want to make an impact. I want to get more stuff done in less time. It's gotten a little easier, but it's definitely still a point of friction. Even before I sit down. I try to justify the fact I shouldn't make time to meditate because I have so many other things that need to get done <u>now</u>. It's about trading what you want the most (being present, calm, and sense of peace) for what you want at the moment.

And many times, what you want at the moment is what you think is going to give you that.

Just getting that one last thing done.

Correcting that one last test, writing that one last blog post, or making that one last phone call or email. But, the thing that took me forever to realize is that there will always be one more thing to do. ALWAYS. The biggest entrepreneurial myth is that we'll get everything done on our to do list. In reality, I probably get 5% of the things done that I actually write down!

It's all about making tradeoffs. I don't even have to go into the fact that every single person reading this book, including myself, could cut out 10 minutes of social media or TV to focus more on our priorities. It's not that you don't have time. It's that it's really not that important to you. It's a choice you have the power to make.

Mental Chatter

Ok. Just focus on your breath. Count one with the inhale and two with the exhale, but only go up to 10 and then start back at one.

"Number one? Who was my favorite player that wore #1? Penny Hardaway. Man, that dude could really play. I saw that ESPN feature on him that he's coaching in Memphis now. I wonder if he'd be interested in helping with DRIVE? Man, I have to reach out to one of our kids. I haven't talked to him for a couple weeks. 27. Argh. I need to start over. 1. 2. 3. Allen Iverson wore number 3. I used to work on his crossover all the time. I remember watching grainy, pixelated videos online of him crossing over Jordan. I bet I've watched that video thousands of times."

This is completely normal. Let go of judgment and get back to the present moment, which is exactly what you need to do in a game, work or life.

Emotions That Arise

The more you meditate, the more you'll feel emotions start to arise. It's perfectly natural to have these come up — even really strong ones that make you want to quit. The key is to be aware of them, sit with them, and they will eventually pass. In order to achieve a deep state of relaxation and focus, you'll have to be able to sit with those emotions. Much longer than you think you should.

Sitting In Lotus Pose

No, you absolutely do not have to sit in the position that I know every single one of you reading this is thinking about right now. I can't sit like that for more than a few minutes. It absolutely kills my hips, so I sit in a chair. The most important thing is to be sitting in an upright position so that you are aware, awake, and alert. You want to sit as if there is a string attached to the top of your head and pulling you up.

CLOSING

HOME WE'LL GO

This book is not about being soft. Actually, quite the opposite. It's about finding our truth, becoming vulnerable, recognizing our gifts, and giving them to the rest of the world. That is tough.

The reason we don't like to talk about our feelings, or simply sit there and be aware of them, is that it is ridiculously hard to do. In this silence, we come closer to the truth. Only in seeking the truth can we find real freedom. Real freedom to make choices that align with where we want to go and who we want to be. And, unless we become aware of our thoughts, we can't find the truth behind what is really driving us. That drive that motivates our decisions each day.

And, those feelings you start to be aware of? Yeah, those are crucial too. Your thoughts influence your feelings and your feelings influence your actions. These actions, continually practiced over time become your habits.

And, your habits.

They determine who you become and what you accomplish. So you literally do become your thoughts.

But, only when we are able to observe our thoughts and feelings can we detach from them. Can we start to see a critical difference — the one between what we perceive and the one that's actually the truth.

No, true toughness isn't ignoring these feelings. Toughness is being able to sit with them and accept them for what they are. Without judgment. Knowing they are only your thoughts and feelings. They do not define you.

Meditation puts us in a position of complete vulnerability. A place where we are completely raw and naked.

A place where we can scrutinize and criticize ourselves for what we feel, what we think, and the actions we take. But, through practice, we become vulnerable because we know we are NOT our thoughts, feelings, and actions. We are the observer. And, as a leader — which is everyone to a certain extent — your ability to influence is directly correlated to your ability to be vulnerable.

The true challenge is that society has built up this definition for us of success. That success, accomplishments, and material things are the key to happiness. Research actually shows a completely different story — that we are happier, not when we <u>achieve</u> things, but when we are <u>present</u>, in a state of flow and working towards our potential at something that we love.

I truly believe that everyone has a unique gift. And that gift is your truest, most authentic self. When we discover this within ourselves we can give it away. And that, I think, is the point of life.

YOU MATTER

I'M NOT. I AM.

I am not my body.

I am not my faults, guilt, or shame.

I am not my anxiety, depression or fears.

And, I am not my thoughts. I am the observer of my thoughts.

The watcher.

My thoughts, my body, and my material things do not define me.

My relationships do not define me.

My accomplishments do not define me.

I transcend all.

I am the author of my own story.

I am the light.

I am the energy.

I am the love.

About The Author

Mike Lee is the founder of Thrive3, a basketball and mindfulness training company, that uses the game to positively influence the lives of middle school through NBA players and coaches. As meditator, yogi and speaker Mike blogs, shares stories and inspires people from across the world to tap into their own personal power through mindfulness.

Un/Train Deeper

To take your experience deeper, visit untrain.com/academy to take our 8 week course.

Speak

To hire Mike to speak at your event, business, school or team contact him at mike@mikeleebasketball.com

Connect On Social

Snapchat whoismikelee
Instagram whoismikelee
Twitter mikeleehoops

References

1. Harris, Dan. *10% Happier: How I Tamed the Voice in My Head, Reduced Stress without Losing My Edge, and Found Self-help That Actually Works: A True Story*. Print. p28

2. Pitino, Rick, and Bill Reynolds. *Success Is a Choice: Ten Steps to Overachieving in Business and Life*. New York: Broadway, 1997. Print. p34

3. Canfield, Jack, and Janet Switzer. *The Success Principles: How to Get from Where You Are to Where You Want to Be*. New York: Harper Resource Book, 2005. Print. p34

4. Achor, Shawn. *The Happiness Advantage: The Seven Principles of Positive Psychology That Fuel Success and Performance at Work*. New York: Broadway, 2010. Print. p38

5. "Good Life Project || Inspiration | Motivation | Happiness | Meaning | Success by Integrity Network on ITunes." *ITunes*. Web. 27 Feb. 2016. p46

6. Chödrön, Pema. *How to Meditate: A Practical Guide to Making Friends with Your Mind*. Print. p50

7. "Get Some Headspace." *Headspace*. Web. 27 Feb. 2016. p50

8. Kabat-Zinn, Jon. *Wherever You Go, There You Are*. London: Piatkus, 2004. Print. p58

9. Osho. *Mindfulness in the Modern World: How Do I Make Meditation Part of Everyday Life?* Print. p58

10. "Pump Up the Jams and Feel Powerful." *Kellogg Insight*. Web. 26 Feb. 2016. p70

11. Maxwell, John C. *Everyone Communicates, Few Connect: What the Most Effective People Do Differently*. Print. p78

12. Maxwell, John C. *Everyone Communicates, Few Connect: What the Most Effective People Do Differently*. Print. p79

13.   Chödrön, Pema. *How to Meditate: A Practical Guide to Making Friends with Your Mind*. Print. p85

14.   Simmons, Russell, and Chris Morrow. *Success through Stillness: Meditation Made Simple*. Print. p86

15.Chödrön, Pema. *How to Meditate: A Practical Guide to Making Friends with Your Mind*. Print.p88

16.   Hardy, Darren. *The Compound Effect: Multiplying Your Success, One Simple Step at a Time*. New York, NY: Vanguard, 2010. Print. p90

17.   Olson, Jeff. *The Slight Edge: Turning Simple Disciplines into Massive Success*. Lake Dallas: Success, 2011. Print. p92

18.   Coyle, Daniel. *The Talent Code: Unlocking the Secret of Skill in Maths, Art, Music, Sport, and Just about Everything Else*. London: Random House, 2009. Print. p93

19.   Achor, Shawn. *The Happiness Advantage: The Seven Principles of Positive Psychology That Fuel Success and Performance at Work*. New York: Broadway, 2010. Print. p93

20.   Medcalf, Joshua, and Jamie Gilbert. *Burn Your Goals: The Counter Cultural Approach to Achieving Your Greatest Potential*. Print. p100

21.   Medcalf, Joshua, and Jamie Gilbert. *Burn Your Goals: The Counter Cultural Approach to Achieving Your Greatest Potential*. Print. p102

22.   Smith, Dean, John Kilgo, and Sally Jenkins. *A Coach's Life*. New York: Random House, 1999. Print.p104

23.   McKeown, Greg. *Essentialism: The Disciplined Pursuit of Less*. Print. p109

24.   Achor, Shawn. *The Happiness Advantage: The Seven Principles of Positive Psychology That Fuel Success and Performance at Work*. New York: Broadway, 2010. Print. p112

25.   Hassler, Christine. *Expectation Hangover: Overcoming Disappointment in Work, Love, and Life*. Print. p113

26. "Befriending Fear: Working with Worry and Anxiety - Mindful." *Mindful.* 2011. Web. 26 Feb. 2016. p116

27. Coyle, Daniel. *The Talent Code: Unlocking the Secret of Skill in Maths, Art, Music, Sport, and Just about Everything Else.* London: Random House, 2009. Print. p125

28. Coyle, Daniel. *The Talent Code: Unlocking the Secret of Skill in Maths, Art, Music, Sport, and Just about Everything Else.* London: Random House, 2009. Print. p126

29. Achor, Shawn. *The Happiness Advantage: The Seven Principles of Positive Psychology That Fuel Success and Performance at Work.* New York: Broadway, 2010. Print. p128

30. Hardy, Darren. *The Compound Effect: Multiplying Your Success, One Simple Step at a Time.* New York, NY: Vanguard, 2010. Print. P136

31. Keller, Gary. *The One Thing.* London, UK: Hachette Book Group, 2013. Print. p140

32. McKeown, Greg. *Essentialism: The Disciplined Pursuit of Less.* Print.p140

33. Maxwell, John C. *Everyone Communicates, Few Connect: What the Most Effective People Do Differently.* Print p146

34. Simmons, Russell, and Chris Morrow. *Success through Stillness: Meditation Made Simple.* Print. p166

35. Hardy, Darren. *The Compound Effect: Multiplying Your Success, One Simple Step at a Time.* New York, NY: Vanguard, 2010. Print. p168

36. Coyle, Daniel. *The Talent Code: Unlocking the Secret of Skill in Maths, Art, Music, Sport, and Just about Everything Else.* London: Random House, 2009. Print. p169

37. Rubin, Gretchen. *The Happiness Project: Or Why I Spent a Year Trying to Sing in the Morning, Clean My Closets, Fight Right, Read Aristotle, and Generally Have More Fun.* New York, NY: Harper, 2009. Print. p173

NAMASTE

CPSIA information can be obtained at www.ICGtesting.com
Printed in the USA
LVOW08s0525290316

481213LV00001B/1/P